ALWAY$ ON $UNDAY

ALWAY$ ON $UNDAY

Jim Klobuchar

with Bud Grant

NODIN PRESS

In Appreciation

The author and Nodin Press wish to thank the *Minneapolis Star Tribune* for permission to reprint selected portions of Jim Klobuchar's writings that appeared originally in the *Star Tribune*, and for permission to reprint photos of Hugh McElhenny's run that appeared originally in the *Star Tribune*.

The Author and Nodin Press thank Ross and Haines publishing, in whose books a small portion of *Always on Sunday* originally appeared.

The author and Nodin Press wish to thank the Minnesota Vikings and its public relations office for making available many of the photos in this book. They also thank the Green Bay Packers for use of photos in this book.

We also wish to thank Jeff Siemon, Jerry Burns, Fran Tarkenton, John Campbell, Matt Birk and Bernie Kukar for their reminiscences that are part of this book.

ISBN 978-1-932472-83-7

Library of Congress Cataloging-in-Publication Data

Klobuchar, Jim.
  Always on Sunday / Jim Klobuchar with Bud Grant.
    p. cm.
  ISBN 978-1-932472-83-7
  1. Football--United States--Anecdotes. 2. Football players--United States--Anecdotes. I. Grant, Bud. II. Title.
  GV954.K47 2009
  796.332--dc22

                              2009024772

Nodin Press, LLC
530 North Third Street
Suite 120
Minneapolis, MN
55401

This book is for Billy Bye, who was a friend to thousands.
He lived every day as a good game just beginning.

Table of Contents

Preface

It's Already Round-the Calendar Show Biz—And Now Favre

By 2009 the expanding mania that is pro football dominated the sports calendar in America to the point where the football millions needed to survive only a few arid weeks between seasons without their daily nourishment of drama and turmoil.

Into this vacuum in early summer stepped the irresistible Brett Favre, having already rescued the nation once, in 2008, when he threw off the shackles of a four-month retirement to sign with the New York Jets. Almost nothing this extraordinary quarterback has done in his career—including his new alliance with the Minnesota Vikings—meets the usual standards of natural law. He played for years with injuries that would have hospitalized Godzilla. He set records for performance and for uninterrupted play, week after week, year after year, that are unlikely to be seriously challenged. By embracing the Jets after retiring from the Packers he accomplished the novel feat of making half of his fans mad at the Packer management and half of them mad at Favre.

The truth of Brett Favre is probably simpler than his annual announcements from someplace in Mississippi, terse and mysterious, suggested. While he is healthy and strong enough to compete, Favre is more than a football lifer. He is eternal youth, or as close to it as we're likely to get. As a reason for his annual reincarnations, one more big payday and revenge against the Packers pale alongside his hunger to extract every joyous and painful moment available to him in football. He has trouble retiring because he can't bear it when he does. In the end, Brett Favre is less to be analyzed than enjoyed. Is he going to take the Vikings to the Super Bowl?

One thing is a cinch. If he does, it will probably lift pro football to an even loftier level—for all the controversy it produces—than it reached a year ago in a Super Bowl climaxed by Pittsburgh's last-breath heroics against the Arizona Cardinals. The replays were still going strong weeks later. Why?

Pro football is sometimes called the ultimate game for America. It gives you speed, violence and skills meshed with wits and a sizable serving of hostility. Add outsized personalities. Add money.

Nobody knows this better than television. It takes ingenuity to escape pro football on TV. This includes periodic scenes in the paddy wagon and night court, gun busts and steroid suspensions. You also get spasms of whacky behavior in the package. The game is big and boisterous but it is also, for millions of people, electric and hard to resist. This book explores the roots of the public's fascination for it and what's different. The personalities by now are in the public domain. So is the game's rhetoric. John Madden's retirement as the Confucius of football analysis was practically bulletin news.

In these atmospherics, Bud Grant's observations are highly relevant. As a retired Hall of Fame coach he applauds the game's success today. He also reminds the National Football League: it owes much of its spreading popularity to its willingness to make changes that moved pro football to the forefront of American sports in a competitive market. He argues that it shouldn't stop now. In this book he proposes a range of changes he believes will heighten the game's appeal to both the stadium audiences and TV watchers. He wants to tighten officiating, dump plays like the fair catch and automatic extra point. He calls them "dead and nothing plays." He wants to open the game even wider and raise the suspense. He also offers some surprising reminiscences of his years with the Vikings that give us an inside look at how he coached, his relations with his players and his values.

Mingled with these are remembrances and comment sifted from one journalist's lengthy involvement with pro football. They reflect the years I covered the game for the Minneapolis newspapers, reaching back to its introduction in Minnesota nearly 50 years ago when its roster was filled with discarded vagabonds and malcontents. They were, ironically, led by a saucy rookie named Francis Tarkenton—and miraculously won their first game. His career ultimately linked those roustabout early years with the Super Bowl teams of the Grant years. Since then, pro football in the 21st Century has taken the game to the stars as a multi billion dollar industry that keeps growing. This book explores both its triumphs and its mounting embarrassments on the police blotter and occasionally on the field. Along the way you'll find stories that gather some of the memorable players and bizarre episodes—from Norm Van Brocklin to Randy Moss and others who have filled the landscape over those years. Among those memories you might also detect a wisp of fondness for another time.

Bud Grant and I met under painful conditions. I remember it in the spirit of forgiveness. He was a three-sport star at the University of Minnesota and in summer pitched for the Superior, Wis. team in an amateur league in 1948. I played shortstop for the Ely, Minnesota, Blu-Sox. The teams met in Superior, his home town. We had men on base in the middle innings. I was batting with two out. Grant had the usual pitching assortment, including the expected high heat, a recognizable curve ball and a menacing demeanor.

I was going to get those runs home one way or another with whatever heroic measures seemed handy. I envisioned a two-run triple. Grant had no inkling of this ambition. His third pitch was a blazer inside. I lost flight of the ball someplace in his uniform or the distant surf of Lake Superior. It hit me high on the right bicep. The runners moved up while I trotted to first. I can tell you now I considered glaring at the pitcher. I dropped that idea when I realized there was a chance we'd meet again in the eighth inning. We lost, but I left with a memento. You can still see the faint stitches of the ball on my right bicep. Our later meetings, as newspaperman and coach, were much more convivial—although not quite always. Call it the nature of the game.

– Jim Klobuchar,
July 2009

1

The Game Now Impossible to Ignore

Television cameras zoomed in on Mike Singletary and he didn't need a cue. He had come to deliver an indictment and he was unstoppable. His text was preening self-centered football players, and he launched each smoldering syllable of disgust with a controlled rage that must have frozen every startled journalist in the interview room.

It outclassed your average tantrum of wrath. This was a scene lifted straight out of biblical times.

The difference was that Mike Singletary was no vengeful voice from the scriptures, although he is an ordained minister. On this day he was the laser-eyed old pro linebacker, a Hall of Famer turned head coach of the San Francisco 49ers, a team in the midst of a mid-season droop. An hour earlier he had evicted Vernon Davis, a tight end who had screwed up by needlessly slapping the helmet of a Seattle player, drawing a 15-yard roughing penalty in the midst of a three-touchdown loss. After being flagged he came back to the bench, revealing no symptoms of penitence or any sign of actually being interested. In the eyes of the fuming coach, Davis was giving him an arrogant slough-off, telling him and the team, "What the hell, between us boys it's just another day and a few thousand bucks more."

Singletary chased him off the field and ordered him to the locker room.

When the game was over Singletary faced the media platoons. He didn't wait for questions. He made a speech, and it was a bombshell. Later that day, when the networks and cables started their round-the-clock reruns on television, millions of viewers gaped. Here was footage they never saw in the post-game comedies featuring Jimmy, Howie, Terry, and the rest of the analytic minions.

Never mind that he was now a coach, and a neophyte head coach at that. No one was ever going to shake the linebacker ferocity out of Mike Singletary. Unless you watched Discovery Channel reruns on Sunday afternoons you had to remember Mike Singletary. He was the Chicago Bears middle linebacker whose eyes drilled the enemy quarterback with electric menace every Sunday, a glare that translated: "If you or anybody comes this way, bodies are going to fly." But on this Sunday in San Francisco he was not only a coach and prosecutor but—as the decibels mounted—the defender of his lodge, the football ethic: "Pro Football As It Should Be Played."

And it was beautiful. Suffering football geeks from coast to coast who resented the All-For-Me mentality soaking into today's pro football were being avenged. His eyes bulged as he spoke.

"I will not tolerate players that think it's about them when it's about the team. We cannot make decisions that cost the team and then come off the field nonchalant. You know what? I'm from the old school. I would rather play with ten people and get penalized down the field until we got to do something else, then play with 11 and know that one of those has not sold out to be a part of this team. It's more about them than the team.

"Cannot play with them.

"Cannot win with them.

"Cannot coach with them.

"Cannot do it.

"I want winners who want to win. I told him (Vernon Davis) he would do a better job for us right now by going and taking a shower than going back on the field.

"That's all."

"It's as simple as that."

Actually, not quite. In his exasperation Mike forgot that you aren't penalized for having less than 11 men on the field.

It didn't matter. It was enough. In a couple of hours it was everywhere on American TV and may even have made it on Al Jazeera. It came a few weeks ahead of the presidential election and it scored higher ratings than Barack Obama and Sarah Palin. In that one surge of fury, the great warhorse spoke for a clientele of 50 or 60 million people. While most them are incurably hypnotized by the round-the-clock merchandised phenomenon that pro football has become today, a lot of them still cling to storybook ideals.

One of those is the concept that John Madden preached as the hallmark of the core athlete—"selling out on every play"—the idea of total commitment of the body and mind. "Bringing it," today's athlete will call it.

Most of them play by that ideal, in a rough sort of way. It's not unknown for a prima donna wide receiver with a $10 million contract to go missing when they call a screen play headed in the other direction, notably when he's carrying a grudge because he was ignored on the last two pass plays. Or he waltzes with the cornerback he's supposed to block. One reason it doesn't happen all that often is that millions of eyes are watching every game the National Football League plays today, plus 22 assistant coaches on your side of the field, plus the high tech cameras that expose all delinquencies at the next team meeting.

But the eruption of delight that Mike Singletary's diatribe set off among pro football's watching hordes was one measure of the game's enormous popularity today. This same popularity can be seen in the torrent of paranoid blogging from the home-grown scholars after their team loses. That and the threatened mutiny of the stadium thousands if the home team blows a game because of what is invariably condemned as "that brainless, stupid no-guts conservative coaching."

Be careful about grooming your precocious 8-year-old to be a head football coach in the National Football League or the big colleges. Better a tight end coach or a sideline reporter. Something sensible and reasonably safe. Coaching today's national anthem contortionists in the rudiments of bearable music might be another.

But head coach? Be careful. Marie Antoinette on her way to the guillotine had it cushy alongside the National Football League coach who loses three in a row.

None of this could be foreseen back in the Middle Ages of pro football and television, the early 1960s, when the National Football League was introduced to the part of the world where I worked as a relatively harmless newspaper writer.

In those years the Minnesota Vikings played in a Toonerville stadium not far from the cornfields of south Bloomington. On the first official appearance of the Minnesota Vikings in a National Football league game in September of 1961 they wore delicate lilac-purple pants that might have been cribbed from the spring fashion show in suburban Orono.

The young quarterback who threw four touchdown passes in his first game as a professional and defeated the Chicago Bears and George Halas—the man who virtually invented pro football—was paid $12,500 for the season.

His name was Francis Tarkenton and nobody saw the game at home because it wasn't televised there. Not a whole lot more saw it in the stadium.

And when it was over the humiliated Bears skulked their way into the team bus for the drive to the airport. Halas boarded a few minutes later and stared savagely into the eyes of his disgraced warriors. Seconds passed. Halas' stare was unforgiving. It mixed contempt with a sense of utter betrayal. More silence. The players, not noticeably repentant, waited for Halas to sit down. But it was now apparent that some kind of judgment was going to be delivered here and the silence was smothering. If he was tempted to give a post-game speech then and there, Halas made no such sign. Finally he offered his spare evaluation of his team and its performance:

"You goddamned pussies!"

Halas sat down and the bus took off.

Singletary never played for Halas, but you had to sense some kind of brotherhood there, although no matter how long Singletary coaches, he's never going to be a serious match for the Stingy Old Bear in creative profanity.

My introduction to pro football, and that of millions of my peers—the Medicare Part D multitudes of today—belongs to the age of Halas and Lombardi, to ankle-high football shoes and black-and-white television. In other words, I've spent a span of better than 50 years watching the sport develop into the extravaganza we have today.

What we see today is a speed-of-light planetarium of sound and flashing images, billionaire owners, millionaire linemen screaming and brawling with millionaire tight ends. We see genuine spectacle and last-second suspense mixed with violence and spasms of grace as well as exhibitionism of the first order. We see gargantuan linemen, fat-gut linemen, touchdown-scoring receivers who run with the speed and agility of cheetahs; multi-million-dollar quarterbacks who can accurately throw a football 70 yards while running a half-step ahead of extinction. We see round-the-clock and round-the-calendar football on television and hordes of otherwise sane businessmen, shoe salesmen, supermarket butchers and college professors pretending to be coaches, totally serious about managing their fantasy football teams, getting tips and instructions from sponsored oracles on television and radio talk shows.

And mostly, America is loving it.

Why? If you saw the 2009 Super Bowl, you have the answer. This was a huge slice of America jammed into four hours. It had tens of millions of people welded to the television set, partying across the country. But the parties yielded to action on the screen. The game between the Pittsburgh Steelers and Arizona Cardinals was drab in the early going, but it developed into a perfect storm of thrust and counter thrust and suspense in a high-stakes clash of athletes playing at the summit levels of their craft and strength. The final minutes lifted the Tampa Bay stadium crowd and the TV millions into a state of intensity nearly unbearable for some of them.

The game was that good. Here were huge men, nimble men, driven in pursuit of the grail of professional football. They hammered each other on every play, sometimes legally. You could see them cursing across the line of scrimmage, trying either to crush or manipulate each other in a multi-million dollar guessing game. For half of the game the stars of both teams were neutralized by the pressures and the strategies. But now the game was coming down to the wire and the playmakers stepped forward—Ben Roethlisberger, James Harrison, Kurt Warner, Larry Fitzgerald and Santonio Holmes.

The fireworks began with an out-of-this-world 100 yard run with an intercepted pass by a heavyweight lineman, James Harrison of the Steelers. He ran as if possessed, clanging indiscriminately off the Arizona pursuers and his own blockers before falling exhausted into the end zone.

At times the entire Steeler secondary seemed fixated on Larry Fitzgerald, the passing-catching prodigy who had begun as a ball boy in the training camp of the Minnesota Vikings. They doubled him downfield on every play. In the second half the Cardinals coaching staff shifted tactics, springing him across the middle, and Fitzgerald caught six passes on one drive, including a leaping grab in the end zone. The game tightened.

Now in the final minutes, the Steelers, who had led almost the entire game, were reeling under the impact of Fitzgerald and quarterback Kurt Warner. So here was Warner, a warrior, a decent man of public service, and an athlete who had risen from the obscurity of the Arena League to earn a Super Bowl ring with the St. Louis Rams. His history was almost a parable, a Superbowl hero who had become something of a football nomad. Now in his late 30s, Warner was returning to stardom with a second team, the up-from-ashes Arizona Cardinals, playing with a demeanor that captivated all who watched him during the Cardinals' zigzag run to the Super Bowl. And here came Fitzgerald with his undefeatable spirit and gymnastic skills. They lit the Cardinals' fire in the dying minutes. And suddenly and remarkably, Arizona was leading.

Jazzed by Bruce Springsteen's halftime acrobatics, the crowd—and probably most of the television audience too—watched that fourth quarter drama with one emotional leap after another.

But the Steelers, who were no strangers to Super Bowl pressure, refused to crumble. In the closing minutes Ben Roethlisberger, a 260-pound quarterback with the physique of a barroom bouncer, was beating the Cardinals blitz, throwing off tacklers and driving the Steelers toward the goal line. With 35 seconds remaining he looked into the end zone. One receiver was covered and a second one, Santonio Holmes drove for the corner and turned. Roethlisberger threw off one more rusher and spiraled the ball high. Holmes lunged, flung his hands over the heads of two defenders, caught the ball and willed himself to stay inbounds. A seemingly endless string of replays from every possible angle confirmed the referee's call on the field—the catch was good. And the Steelers won the Super Bowl.

This was pro football, the National Football League, at the zenith. For all of its embarrassment over steroids, night club shootings and rap sheets, there is nothing on the American sports scene that can quite compare with the ongoing public phenomenon that professional football is today. The reason isn't hard to divine. It's a game made for, and freely promoted by the mass audiences of today's television. It is a quintessential American game: It couples violence with speed and nerve, and mixes collisions with artfulness. It's a concussive chess match of driven players witnessed not only in the arenas but in millions of living rooms. There the home dwellers know the names, know the numbers, know some of the mumbo-jumbo of the game's rhetoric—the Cover 2 pass defenses, the empty backfield, the 7 in the box or the 8 in the box, the gadget play. They may squirm with the dead time taken by the not-so instant replay. But its hooded mysteries and obscure sight angles create millions of TV-watching juries who pass judgment from the comfort of their living rooms. Which means everybody gets into the action in an audience-participation parlor game.

And this creates a massive American community watching the game from ocean to ocean, in living rooms as well as the stadiums, plus armies more crowding the sports bars and some, well, in the bedroom.

It's a different game today, and the atmospherics have radically changed from the days when the Minnesota Vikings, for example, entered the league. In those years Norm Van Brocklin, the first Viking coach, was criticized for installing the first Viking training camp in Bemidji, in the heart of Minnesota's primeval forests. A sports editor of the time wrote that 300 miles from the Minneapolis-St. Paul metropolis was too far from the communication centers to give the Vikings adequate publicity.

"Publicity, hell," Van Brocklin snarled. "With the 36 stiffs I've got we need cover and concealment, not publicity."

He may have been right. In the early 1960s television tolerated pro football,

Coach Norm Van Brocklin and quarterback Fran Tarkenton

wasn't really sure what to do with it. There were some executives who thought *Masterpiece Theater* was a better draw. Today it's a multi-billion dollar partnership. Game officials synchronize with the television networks in scheduling timeouts. A shot of the billionaire owner offering a photo op is also pretty much de rigueur on the TV networks. He is seen entertaining his rich friends, or seized by anxiety in his stadium suite or, if it's Jerry Jones of Dallas, patrolling the sideline importantly.

In its partnership with TV, the pro football's ownership now forms a very plush club. It's a love match of megabucks investors and mutual backscratchers who share the profits and have been smart enough to let professionals like Peter Rozelle, Paul Tagliabue and Roger Goodell run a tight ship. For millions, the entertainment and story lines of pro football are hard to resist and TV heightens the suspense. Occasionally the dog and pony shows of the analyst panels are more entertaining than the action. Sometimes they turn slapstick, although the talking heads are rarely given enough time to impart meaningful inside information. The viewer usually forgives, because the experts in the announcing booths and panel shows do add a dynamic to what the TV audience used to watch. If television has made major advances in seriously educating the fan and mass audiences in the last two or three decades—apart from the technological advances in camera work—it is essentially there. The Troy Aikmans, Jaws Jaworskis, and Phil Simms' are an integral part of the show today, where there were practically none of that breed in the earliest years of televised pro football.

Is football, in fact, TOO big? Possibly. Is the product maxed out? Or can it be improved? At least one of its most respected old warriors, Bud Grant, thinks it can, particularly if the league employs full-time professional officials. Is that in the future?

And if it is, is that progress?

2

A Wise Old Coach Says
Winning May Be Harder Today

In the win-or-die stages of the 2008 National Football League season in early December, showdown games for the playoffs blanketed the television sets of America. And with big money and prestige on the line in the most glamorous sport in the country, a series of events was also transpiring *off* the field as a bizarre sideshow to the primetime weekend package. Among the highlights:

• The star receiver of the New York Giants, Plaxico Burress, shot himself in the leg in a night club and the next day was driven to court in handcuffs for carrying a concealed weapon without a permit while the cops tried to figure out why they were the last to learn about it. He was gone for the rest of the season and the defending Super Bowl champion Giants blew the playoffs.

• In Dallas, crowds cheered, more or less, as a cornerback named Adam (Pacman) Jones, freshly rehabilitated after a loony assault on his own bodyguard, donned a Dallas Cowboys uniform once more. His rejuvenation came after his year-long suspension for involvement in a shooting on the West Coast. At the time, the gunshot event competed for headlines with the conviction of Atlanta quarterback Michael Vick for hosting a multi-million dollar dog-fighting ring. Pacman's dramatic reform briefly upstaged Terrell Owens in Dallas, which was once considered an impossible feat. But Owens launched a comeback by confiding that he'd heard rumors accusing quarterback Tony Romo of conspiring to ignore him in the next game and drawing up a personal game plan featuring Romo's roommate, Jason Witten, as the primary receiver.

• A few days later, the Cowboys released Pacman, evidently without discussing it with Terrell Owens. After all of these creative preliminaries, Dallas managed to defy all odds by dropping three of its last four games and missing the playoffs. Two months later, after being evicted by Dallas, Owens was revealed as the latest savior of the Buffalo Bills, and promptly proclaimed Buffalo the most marvelous land on earth.

• In St. Paul, in the wake of Plaxico Burress, Pacman Jones and Terrell Owens, lawyers for the National Football League and the players' association argued against the suspension of a half dozen players who were said to have taken steroid-masking diuretics in violation of the league-player agreement.

Two of them formed the unsinkable fortress of the Minnesota Viking defense, Pat and Kevin Williams. Earlier in the week, the NFL had announced that these two were to be suspended for the last four games of the regular season. Viking fans groaned in unison. Coach Brad Childress unhappily probed his roster. The team was winning again but hanging on by its thumbs in the struggle for a berth in the NFL playoffs.

How do you replace the best two-man defensive front in football? Basically you can't. You begin by conscripting the two last survivors of the roster cuts and then working the beads hard. It went that way for three days. Late in the week lawyers for the players got a temporary restraining order to stop the suspension. On Friday, two days before a big game in Detroit, a judge in St. Paul delayed the suspension until he could sort out the mess. The Williams' played. The Vikings defeated winless Detroit with a fourth quarter rally. Somebody suggested giving the game ball to the judge.

Somewhere on his way home from his hunting cabin in northern Wisconsin, Harry Peter (Bud) Grant was sifting through all these amazements of 21st century professional football life.

"You know," he said, "it would be difficult for me to coach professional football today."

You'll note he didn't say he couldn't. Grant is a conservative man with the language but he rarely sacrifices clarity. He wasn't saying the pro football extravaganza of today is a kind of game he doesn't remember coaching. In fact, he believes the game has avoided pitfalls that might have lessened it. Nor was he saying it doesn't deserve the record audiences it has assembled on television and in the stadiums.

He WAS saying that his kind of coaching might not be the best fit for 21st Century in the comfort level he achieved from it and the results that followed.

Hearing that remark, Grant's quarterback of the 1970s, Hall of Famer Francis Tarkenton, howled an objection. "Grant," he said, "could coach in the Sahara or on Greenland Ice Cap and beat you four out of five either place."

But when Grant coached—the last year was in 1985 when he was the highest paid coach in the NFL-- football players didn't campaign from their websites for more playing time or publicly lobby their coach for more touches inside the red zone.

Fifty years ago a clubby but largely old-school platoon of NFL owners gathered in Florida to chart a new television policy with the new and young commissioner, Pete Rozelle. Rozelle swung pro football's first big contract with network television and set the NFL on its high-speed course to prosperity. At the time, they could scarcely have imagined the colossus that the game is today. Nor could they have imagined the jazzed multitudes who would watch it in the stadiums, in their homes, in sports bars and in the back seats of their cars; or imagined the cult atmosphere it has fostered.

Still, there are a few lesser millions who remember a game not quite as fashionable and multi-layered as the pro football of today. Then, TV ads at halftime told men what to wear and how to avoid falling hair. Today half of them tell you how to acquire an erection.

This is probably progress, although it may never replace marching bands. Those were blissful years when a linebacker didn't behave like a circus acrobat and somersault down the field in jubilation after making a tackle for a two yard loss. Hare-brained sideshows are now accepted as part of the game and usually force elders in the crowd as well as the press box to go to great lengths not to sound like old crocks. Why? Well, today's game is, after all, a new and jazzy pro football. Rock and roll guitar pickers bring us to the kickoff, if we can see it through the smoke bombs. The national anthem takes five minutes to wind down, although the singer occasionally finishes on key even when the words are wailed instead of sung and sometimes completely forgotten.

But it truly IS faster football, exquisitely produced and formatted. It is a football played by uniformly better athletes, bigger and richer players, text-messaging players and YouTube players. It is also played by 350 pound linemen—who also are demonstrable athletes and versatile, as adept doing the tango on a television show as they are smothering a draw play.

That is the perception of today's pro football, and all of these things are more or less true.

And yet it will be a gloomy day when the flash of today's game begins to dull our memories, at least mine, of Walter Payton and Jim Brown, of John Unitas and Joe Montana, Dick Butkus and Big Daddy Lipscomb, Sam Huff and Geno Marchetti, Raymond Berry and Alan Page, and the notorious thigh-biting Conrad Dobler, about whom more later. So it might be a service to today's mingled football generations to scan the faces and times that linked the eras, explore what made them different and to probe the game's future.

Harry Peter (Bud) Grant was invited as a guide into this hairy wilderness. No one is better qualified. Grant took Minnesota Viking football out of the muskeg swamps of its beginnings and into the Arcadia of the Super Bowl. For two decades he was the face of Minnesota football, headset strapped over his billed cap on the sideline, standing motionless in the midst of the pouring snowflakes. Behind him his players jumped up and down to keep warm on the sidelines, hands inside their belts where a few of them had secreted contraband handwarmers. They were brave but they silently envied the lucky stiffs on the opponents' bench, who had 50-horsepower heaters blowing the ice off their noses and the numbness out of their hands.

The sight of hot air blowers on the sideline of a football field personally offended Bud Grant. They were not only a distraction but interfered with the laws of nature. Nobody on the Viking bench complained. It wasn't done. If it's cold, Bud Grant said, you're going to be cold. Accept it. After that, ignore it. You're not going to die. Play our game. The other guys hate the cold. They don't want to be out of there. They took three and out and headed back to the heat blowers.

From the University of Minnesota campus, where he played Big Ten football and basketball, Grant moved on to the play pro football with the Philadelphia Eagles and the Winnipeg Blue Bombers, pro basketball with the old Minneapolis Lakers, and to coach in Winnipeg

Bud Grant during his college years at the University of Minnesota

24

when he retired as player. There he won four championship Grey Cups before he came to the Minnesota Vikings as the head coach, succeeding Norm Van Brocklin. From 1966 to 1985 he took the Vikings to the Super Bowl four times, won 11 division titles, three conference championships, one National Football League championship and ultimately was inducted into the NFL Hall of Fame.

He passed 80 not long ago but there are two places where you're not likely to miss him—in the duck blinds or his windowed office in the headquarters campus of the Minnesota Vikings. He has maintained a consultant's office there since he retired from active coaching. It's honorary, of course, but also a little more than that, which may explain why Bud Grant won more games per season than almost any coach in NFL history. He coached undramatically but there never was a question about the source of the discipline that characterized his teams. From the beginning he had the game hunter's shrewd understanding that the opportunities of life usually don't just happen but basically need to be created. He retired in 1983. His successor won all of three games in 1984. The year was a shambles. The season ticket holders were rebellious and the Vikings' Mike Lynn, the general manager, implored him to come back. Grant considered. Well, yes, he said. A good contract? Right. And it would be nice, he said, after he finally did retire, to have an office and an annual honorarium.

"In perpetuity?" the suits inquired.

Well, something close to that.

The suits looked at the 1985 schedule and the season ticket prospects.

"Done," they said.

He coached in 1985, a middling season, and decided his first impulse was right in 1983. So he retired again and became an unofficial consultant. Today he hunts and fishes, campaigns for cleaner water and spends days with his large and remarkable family. His wife, Pat, was an extraordinary woman with a sense of joy and volunteerism who managed a family of six children plus her husband's dogs when he was at the ball yard. She died in March of 2009, mourned by thousands beyond her family. None of their six children and numerous grandchildren live more than a 30-minute drive from the parental home in Bloomington, MN. He renews his friendships and frequently drives to his office to talk football with friends or football people who visit, sometimes with the present-day Viking entourage.

We were not exactly strangers. I wrote pro football for the Minneapolis newspapers in different shifts from the early 1960s to the championship seasons of the 70s and a little beyond. We visited from time to time after the '80s to renew good times, including a day when we'd talked for a half hour before a horrendous cackling filled the room. "Gawd," I said, "did something fly in through the window?"

Grant laughed conspiratorially. "No, that's my clock. Up there on the wall. Every hour on the hour you get a different sound from the woods. That was your typical North American pheasant. If you stayed long enough you'd get a loon or a snow goose or maybe something bigger."

But there were no hot air blowers here. We talked football and the game today.

"You know," he said, "there's a lot that's different about how the game is played, but that wouldn't be the real difference for me—then and today. The structure of the teams is different today. Players move. The salaries are huge compared with what they were, and more power to the players if they can become millionaires. But you have salary caps today and more mobility for the players. The players making big money are likely to be more protective, or their agents are, although you still have a lot of guys who make big money who lay it on the line on every play. You still have guys who would run through walls. The point is, when I coached it was easier to keep your core players together year after year. The key to all of that was picking the right guys for the long haul. I always thought I was more a builder than a coach. Because I played so many positions—tight end, linebacker, defensive end and a lot more, I had an advantage, I think, in evaluating young players at different positions and developing them into reliable veterans, who are usually the winners."

Ron Yary, Ed White, and Mick Tinglehoff

He would say incessantly, "There is ability and there is durability. One can get you by for a while. But if you're not durable, all the ability you began with isn't going to help build a full career.

When Grant coached, an even larger word was continuity, which is a luxury in big time football today with its free agency, salary caps, escalating salaries and alarming increase in disabling injuries. When Grant coached, his staff of assistants didn't roll over if his team didn't make the playoffs. He hired coaches who worked easily with him and the players—Jerry Burns, John Michels, Bob Hollway, Neil Armstrong, Jocko Nelson, Buster Mertes. His players stayed for most of their careers—Jim Marshall, Carl Eller, Alan Page, Ron Yary, Jeff Siemon, Wally Hilgenberg, Mick Tinglehoff, Ed White, Bill Brown, Joey Browner, Roy Winston, and Lonnie Warwick and others who played for his title teams.

Having Jim Finks as the team's general manager through the heart of Grant's stewardship immensely added to its stability. Finks was a winner, shrewd but companionable, a smart and decent man who never changed his value systems despite the pressures.

Grant isn't bothered by the salary levels in pro football today. Football is a hard and sometimes dangerous game and the competition to play in it is ferocious. The money the game has produced both directly and indirectly runs into the billions of dollars. The big income players are high profile TV stars, not only on Sundays but around the clock from August to February. Stardom in the game can be a quick bridge to long term income and visibility on TV. But the down side is that no player, star or mediocrity, is more than one play removed from losing it all to injury or to a silly decision in a night club.

"There were more things a coach could control when I was doing it," he said. "We chose young players pretty well, and we developed and stayed with them. We tried to avoid players we thought were selfish or prima donnas. The ones we kept got the same coaching year after year. The teamwork that developed is something you can't very well buy. We had different personality types but we had a team that was pretty much together. We had players from the warm weather states who made their homes here year-round. That's not very common today."

But the exhibitionism that the old guard so detests in today's game wasn't exactly unknown in Grant's years.

"No, but we, well discouraged it, pretty successfully. It's another reason I'm not sure I'd love coaching today. Today you've got guys making the tackle on a kickoff and then running 25 yards up the field so the cameras can chase them, and these guys aren't even on the first teams. It's so common today that it's become part of the entertainment, although it was worse when they did the group dances in the end zone." The league outlawed the most garish forms of celebration a while back, although the sackers still pound their chests and figure out a way to cut out 20 feet of space and play Superman for the TV audience.

It's not as though Grant's teams were immune to that kind of spectacle.

The name of Sammy White is imperishable in the archives of Minnesota Vikings, in part because of a behavioral trauma he experienced playing for Harry Peter Grant. In fact, that episode became a mini-saga nationally for a day or so, after which good will pretty much flowed all around.

Sammy was an agreeable and chatty little guy who came out of Grambling College in Louisiana as a wide receiver. He had speed, hands, heart and a finger-snapping love of life. He quickly became a favorite of Francis Tarkenton, the veteran quarterback whose disposition was not all that different from Sammy's, although it was always under control.

Sammy White hauls down a pass.

The Vikings were headed for their fourth Super Bowl in 1976. Sammy made the varsity and was paired with Ahmad Rashad as the Vikings' outside receiving threats. Chuck Foreman was the running back. Page, Eller. Paul Krause, Jeff Siemon and Marshall were the defensive stars. Nate Wright and Wally Hilgenberg were there, and the Detroit Lions—a team that actually won football games in that era—came into old Metropolitan Stadium for a nationally-televised game. The Lions blitzed Tarkenton on almost every down. That was the game plan. Tarkenton loved it. "They blitz," he told the huddle, "and we throw downfield. They blitz and we're going to win."

It helped to have Yary and Ed White and Mick Tinglehoff and Chuck Foreman picking off the blitzers. It was Russian Roulette all day, the big and speedy Detroit blitzers against the Viking blocking scheme, Tarkenton's savvy and quick release, and Sammy White and Rashad running deep. At a critical point in the second half the Lions sent their red dogs against Tarkenton once more. Tarkenton bought three seconds of time and then threw to Sammy White, who was racing down field a step ahead of Levi Johnson. The Met crowd of 46,000, seeing the separation, began to roar as the ball spiraled toward Sammy.

It was a crescendo when the ball settled into Sammy's sure hands. He raced toward the goal line two strides ahead of Johnson and then, ten yards from the goal line, triumphantly lifted the ball above his head. Johnson was gone but the Lions' great Lem Barney, racing crossfield, wasn't. Barney dove, stretched out, and grabbed Sammy's foot. Sammy stumbled and the ball, now loose, dribbled into the end zone, where Levi Johnson of the Lions fell on it for a touchback. No points.

Sammy White, rookie receiver, gathered himself for the long jog across the field to the Vikings' bench, where Coach Bud Grant, the dedicated enemy of exhibitionism on the football field, stood expressionless, his headset strapped over his bill cap.

Sammy was thinking at this moment, very hard. "That play," he said later, "I was feeling so good. I wanted to dance and sing. I knew I was about to score so I just held the ball up. I wasn't going to spike it. Then I felt myself tripped and the ball went into the end zone and the other guy beat me to it. Man, I didn't want to go back to the bench. I figured something terrible was going to happen to me. I'm going to be fired or something worse."

The coach motioned to Sammy White, who came over to listen, his life passing before him.

"Sammy," Grant said. "There's show biz in football. But there's a difference between showbiz and showboating."

Silence.

"You'll get another chance," the coach said.

With three minutes left and the Vikings nursing a thin lead, Sammy White lined up on the outside again. The Lions were going to blitz. Sammy was talking to himself. If anybody could bail him out, it was Tarkenton. Francis was his football patron and his mentor and refuge. He was saying, "Francis, please throw me the ball, just one more time." The lines collided and Sammy White came off the blocks. It was Levi Johnson again. Sammy gave him a shoulder and hip and sprinted diagonally across the field. Tarkenton's bodyguards held off the Lion blitz. He lofted the ball deep. Like a delinquent waif sensing redemption, Sammy pulled the ball down and loped into the end zone for the clinching touchdown. He did not hold the ball in the air. He did not hula as he approached the goal. What he did was carry the ball with two hands and give it politely to the official. The crowd howled. Later, in the locker room, Tarkenton made a speech, and then took a ball and re-enacted Sammy's epic scene, the stumble, Sammy's disgrace—and with the players laughing and applauding—handed the game ball to the young receiver.

A few hours later Sammy received a telephone call from home. His mother was on the line, having seen the game.

"Son," she said, "what did you learn today?"

Sammy explained what he had learned.

The next voice was his father's.

"Son," he said, "will you kindly tell me what you were thinking of when you held that ball in the air."

Sammy obediently explained that whatever was going on in his mind wasn't enough.

And later the young receiver thanked the coach who might have benched him, but instead gave him the world's shortest lecture and said he would get another chance.

Two months later Sammy was voted the NFL Rookie of the Year.

3

A Super Bowl Referee
Invites You Under the Hood

In his suburban Minneapolis home last December, an athletic-looking man in his 60s from Minnesota's Iron Range sat watching the Sunday afternoon dramatics with more careful scrutiny than your average nacho-munching TV viewer.

The action on the screen was from Baltimore—the replay of one of the most controversial moments of the 2008 NFL season. The referee materialized from under the instant replay hood in the final minute of the game and announced a decision that made him an overnight villain in Baltimore in the same league as Robert Irsay, who moved the Colts to Indianapolis in the dead of night in 1984.

The interested migrant from the Iron Range on that December Sunday was Bernie Kukar, out of football now but for years one of the ranking officials in the National Football League and the referee in two Super Bowl games—the assignment that goes to the highest-graded of all NFL referees. We'll probe the candid thoughts of this official-in-retirement in a few moments, and slip with him under that notorious hood. What he has to say will give you some surprises.

You may have seen parts of the game, one of the most brutal in recent memory. Night was falling with the Pittsburgh Steelers trailing the Baltimore Ravens 9-6 in the final minutes of a battle for the playoffs, when Ben Roethlisberger launched the Steelers' desperation drive. The goal line was 92 yards away. And here it gets eerie. The situation facing the Steelers was almost identical to the setting of the

Super Bowl two months later, almost to the yard, to the minute, to the two key players involved and to the outcome.

The Ravens defense, with the relentless linebacker Ray Lewis goading and driving it on every play, wasn't going to give the Steelers much on the ground, and there were only a few minutes left on the clock, so Big Ben threw. On the money. Play after play. The Ravens came hard. He kept throwing. The Steelers moved down field and with 43 seconds left reached the 4 yard line. It was third down. Think Super Bowl once more. Roethlisberger wants to throw, only this time it's against the Ravens and not the Cardinals, as it would be in February.

The roar of the Baltimore crowd was a tidal wave, but the Steelers snapped the ball on time and Roethlisberger dropped back again. The receivers fanned out and the rushers powered in on Roethlisberger. He moved left, scanning the end zone under the pressure. And now Santonio Holmes came open just beyond the goal line—the same Santonio Holmes who a few weeks later leaped high in the final seconds to win the Super Bowl against Arizona. But this was Baltimore, and Roethlisberger pulled the trigger. With both feet in the end zone, Holmes leaned forward to protect the ball as it spiraled into his hands, hard. The ball and his hands were at the goal as he caught it, falling forward.

The linesman signaled no touchdown. It didn't matter that his feet were in the end zone. The ball had to be there, too.

The ball was going to be placed inches short of the goal line, leaving the Steelers with a decision to go for it on the final play to win, or to kick a field goal to tie.

There was no way on earth that this play was going to escape a review, and Walt Coleman went under the hood in that sanctum sanctorum of today's pro game, the replay booth. He sifted through every angle of the play available to him from the network feed. It was terrific theater. Millions in the TV audience joined the Baltimore crowd immersed in the tension. Coleman emerged as undramatically as he could, but he must have been ready for the crowd's explosion.

The play, he said, was a touchdown. The decision on the field was overturned.

He got the explosion. And a few moments later the game was over. Pittsburgh wins and the circus begins in what would become a non-stop, round the clock highlight reel triggering noisy quarrels on the panel shows, which normally end when Terry Bradshaw accuses Jimmy Johnson of changing his hair stylist. But this one was big time. It demanded a decision on the spot, and Walt Coleman didn't duck it.

What Coleman had seen was at least one image showing the point of the football covering a slice of the goal line if it were extended upward. This was just before Santonio Holmes toppled out of the end zone into the field of play. In the words of the football lectionary, the ball had "crossed the plane of the goal line." That's all that was needed for an overturn and for a touchdown.

In the NBC studio where the network's board of analytic prowess was preparing for the Sunday night game to follow, Cris Collinsworth convened a kangaroo court of review during Coleman's vigil in the booth. His fellow jurists were Bob Costas, the moderator, Dan Patrick on leave from radio and Keith Olbermann, on leave from his aerie as chief prosecutor of the Bush administration at MSNBC.

Collinsworth, a onetime star receiver in the NFL and one of its shrewdest TV commentators, is a legitimate football expert. When John Madden retired as the resident wise man of NBC's Sunday Night Football a few months later, the network wasted no time in naming Collinsworth his successor. In that disputed call in Baltimore Collinsworth functioned as the foreman of the jury. The others, Costas, Patrick and Olbermann, are knowledgeable and popular sports broadcasters dedicated to the Pursuit of Truth as well as entertainment. "Indisputable evidence" to overturn a decision on the field they agreed, was the holy of holies of the replay. And they didn't see any thing on the reruns to overrule the linesman's call of no touchdown.

But Coleman came out of the booth and ruled it a touchdown, and he wasn't bashful about it.

The controversy played out all night and spilled over into the wee hours of the talk shows' graveyard shift.

The next day a spokesman for the National Football league's head of officials, Mike Pereira, agreed with the referee's overturn.

"Walt Coleman determined via high-def review that the receiver had possession and two feet down with the ball on the goal line, meaning it broke the plane."

Meaning the league's boss of officials supported the call of the game referee, and did it emphatically.

I called Kukar a little while later. "That support Coleman got from the chief of officials," I asked, "is that part of the good ole boys network, taking care of each other's backside?"

"Nothing of the kind," Kukar said. "When an important call is wrong in the judgment of the people in New York, they'll say so. That's been my experience. You saw the call in Baltimore. What did you think?"

I thought Coleman got it right in reversing the call and ruling it a touchdown."

"So did I," Kukar said. "There was one frame in those images he was looking at, the same one we saw on television, where the point of the ball was touching the line. He saw that, and the official linesman who made the initial call didn't have the benefit of that view. It's what Coleman had to do."

Bernie Kukar has the sound and appearance of a man comfortable with his performance at the highest level of the official's craft. On two of his fingers are the hard-to-ignore emblems of the ultimate respect conferred on his work as an NFL official, the jumbo Super Bowl diamond rings awarded to the game referee. It was pressure, but he enjoyed it. And there were days when the antics of a Warren Sapp would practically break him up in the middle of a game and provoke a running banter between the two.

He is also aware that at least one prominent man in the coaching lodge, Minnesota's Bud Grant, has been stubbornly crusading for years for the professionalization of NFL officials, making the job of officiating their primary source of income.

Grant's argument: "They do it in pro baseball, basketball and other major professional games. In pro football you'll get a guy who is CEO of a bank for five days and then flies in to work the game on weekends and on Monday he goes back to his office to be a CEO again."

Grant wants officials to see football as the players and coaches see it, the midweek practices, each official assigned to a team different from the one he will be working with on game day.

What would that accomplish?

"It would make them more alert," Grant insists. "They'd see it full speed in practice which, means, incidentally, that they ought to be young enough to keep up. A lot of the officials in the league are too old, and shouldn't be out there. What the league needs is career football officials, staying on top of changes in the game. They should spend some of their midweek time getting conditioned to how the players react to different situations, the techniques the players use. That's going to help them when they're in the middle of the action on game day. It's going to help in calling penalties or not calling penalties.

Bernie Kukar has heard the argument. He's not offended by it. Grant is one of the football people he respects. All the same, he doesn't agree.

Kukar's rebuttal runs like this:

"Football teams play one game a week. We officiate one game a week. It's why pro football doesn't especially need officials to be careerists. I don't know what the proficiency level was in the earlier days of pro football. But today an official who makes it to the NFL has been scouted, evaluated, tested and worked out for years. They're scouted in all of the college conferences and now the Arena League. And they have to be in physical shape and stay in shape. I'm typical. I ran miles to make sure I was on top of the game physically. Most of the officials in the NFL today began as part-time officials in high school leagues, small college leagues, then in major college football. They came out of other work venues or businesses and officiated on the side for the extra money in it and because the excitement and demands of officiating appealed to them. And then because they were good at it they attracted better officiating jobs and the extra money supplemented their regular income significantly."

It's the path Kukar followed after he left his native Gilbert on Minnesota's Mesabi Range to study and play football at St. John's in Collegeville, Minnesota. Eventually he went into business with the old Control Data company, then into insurance, and ultimately he became owner of a boy's camp in northern Minnesota.

By the time he came to the attention of the NFL scouts, he was officiating in the North Central Conference and other leagues. He was hired by the NFL in 1984.

"When I was hired, newer officials were getting around $450 a game. Obviously you couldn't make a living doing that. Of course it's gone higher now with the popularity of the game and the increased revenue it's generating. NFL officials today can make from $2,300 to $8,000 a game depending on longevity and whether they earn promotion to the ranks of a referee. They're guaranteed 15 league games out of the 16-game schedule. Referees work almost full time, watching film, preparing reports, consulting with league officials, attending meetings, grading members of their officiating team, sometimes arguing with New York about the grades given to officials on their team.

"I'm not sure spending two or three days watching a team practice would add to our awareness or preparation for the coming game. We're certainly not going to be watching the team that's playing in the next game we officiate. I don't know any coach who would want or allow that. And after all the games we see, the talks we have and the films we check, I don't think there's any mystery about the playing habits of the players in the NFL. We're familiar with the headhunters around the league and all of the moves of the cornerbacks and the DNA of the rushers and pass blockers."

But Kukar understands Grant's point of view. Coaches and game officials don't nurture a mutual love and trust growing deeper through time. A bonehead call by an official is inevitably going to create serious umbrage in a coach whose livelihood depends on winning football games. And with millions of TV viewers watching the replays, it's more important than ever that the officials get it right.

Which is why the instant replay was not only introduced as an official tool on the field, but touted by its enthusiasts as a wonder cure for those bad-call or no-call episodes that were embarrassing the league and costing the victims playoff berths and big money.

Its first trial was a bust because it took too long, and the fans rebelled against this clumsy mystery theater that seemed to attract ridicule and anger at a level embarrassing to the league. It often infuriated the fans and drove some of the coaches to the door of intensive care. That's an impressive collage of victims. So after three years the replay was back, dressed up with the coaches' challenge system to limit its use and to add another element of decision-making and strategy to the coach's role. The 60 second time limit on a decision was another primary improvement.

Instant Replay has now been accepted by almost all of its former critics. What happens now when the referee disappears under that dark cloth to render judgment with the outcome of a game suddenly in jeopardy because of a disputed catch in the end zone? For millions of watchers it's an agonizing sixty seconds, heavily laden with foreboding. The melodrama can get pretty thick, evoking something close to one of those scenes out of the Middle Ages when the black-masked executioner comes out of the shadows swinging an ax. Here it's the referee with a headset and a microphone switch on his hip, announcing. "The call on the field is reversed. The receiver had both feet in bounds and the result is a touchdown."

Mass depression strikes the wounded multitudes, and delirium overcomes the others. The instant replay wasn't contrived to be raw theater, but on some days it's the culminating act. Pete Rozelle, the NFL's first commissioner of pro football's television era, couldn't have dreamed up a piece of drama more suspenseful—and one that also happens to make it a better game.

Bernie Kukar escorts us into the booth. "We'd have one of our NFL staff up in the televisions booths feeding us the network takes on a play. I'd be talking to him. Let's say it's a play about having control of the ball as the receiver is knocked out of bounds. Did he have the ball in possession inbounds before he lost it on the way down. They'd freeze the action that figures in the play. I'd say give me the side shot. Then, OK, let it run natural speed. Or bring it down frame by frame. Now give me the other shot, the other side. And now the screen would go blank for a few seconds. And I haven't got the defining shot yet. You've got 60 seconds. I'd worry about running out of time. That's what happens a lot of times when the referee comes out of booth and says "the ruling on the field stands." There may have been a clear view that either supports or overturns the ruling on the field. But I never got to that frame because time was running out. And let's say the TV audience has seen the defining frame. But there wasn't enough time while I was looking at the other frames. So the fan in the living room is going to ask himself, 'What's he looking at? It was plain as day.' It may have been, but the referee never saw the right angle. That doesn't happen often. Usually the officials get it right on replay. But it does happen.

"After I retired, people would ask me whether it was tough dealing with the pressure, with millions of people in the TV audience and the home crowd ready to hammer you if the call went against their team. I tell them, "When you've been in this for 43 years, 22 of them in the NFL, you've seen everything there is to see. What about this play and that play? I tell them the referee's main job is to lead the team of officials, but the other big part is to watch the quarterback and the action around the quarterback—is he outside the tackle box when he throws the ball away to avert a sack? Watch for hits to the head, helmet to helmet, late hits. I don't know what's going on further down the field. So let's say one of the guys down field throws the flag on a deep pass. I run 50 yards downfield as fast as I can and ask him, "What have you got?" and he says pass interference on the defense Number 22. I get the details from him and announce it to the crowd and get ready for the boos if Number 22 is their guy.

"The crowds are interesting. Sometimes you'll get a game that drones on and on, lot of punts, nothing much happening and the crowd is falling asleep. So sometimes I had a little fun. I'd leave my mike on and blow the whistle hard and suddenly thousands of people sit up and look around to see what happened, and they're not quite sure but they sure are back in the game."

Call it Confessions of a Zebra. The game, in fact, might be a whole lot more interesting if the crowd could eavesdrop on some of the dialogue between the head zebra and the coaches and players.

"One of my favorite coaches," Kukar said, "was Brian Billick when he coached the Baltimore Ravens. Billick never met a TV camera he didn't like. We had a lot of fun. When there was a questionable play or call, or what he decided was a questionable call, he'd wave me over to the sideline. The first thing I'd do would be to ask him, 'Billick, is there a cameraman somewhere around?' I asked him that because there always was. He'd laugh but he always had some kind of scheme. So I'd say, 'what are you going to do while that camera guy is near, yell at me?' And he'd say, 'Yeah, I'm going to yell at you.' And I'd say, OK, but don't make it too loud or too long.'

"In other words, OK, 'I'm going to give you a few seconds of TV time and then you have to shut up.' Which he did.

"The only thing I knew for sure was that it wasn't going to be the last time. Billick was a good coach but also a funny guy. Tell you a story. Baltimore and Tennessee were locked up in a big Monday Night game late in the season when both were fighting for playoff position. Tennessee was down by a few points and moving for what might be the winning touchdown late in the game. They can win if they score and kick the extra point. They complete a pass down around the 2 yard line with seconds left. Players rushed to get into position. It was a real prison break. They sorted themselves out, Tennessee ran the play and went in for a touchdown. My head linesman comes running up. I ask him what he's got. He says he's got offsides on the defense, meaning Baltimore. I said OK, I'll announce it. "The defense was offside, the play results in a touchdown."

But—

"After the announcement the line judge comes running over and says, 'I think we've got a problem here. When the defense was rushing to get lined up, I think the defensive guy pushed the quarterback as he was running to line up.' That would mean encroachment on the defense and negate the play. So that penalty rubs out the call of offsides on the defense because once the encroachment took place, it nullified anything that happened later. In other words, there would be no play. And the Tennessee crowd is already going wild because they think they've scored.

"And I told the line judge, 'You know, I think you're right. I saw this guy coming into the quarterback. But the head linesman who called offside before Tennessee went into the end zone couldn't have seen it. The line judge stuck with his view. So I had to go over and tell Jeff Fisher, the Tennessee coach, what we had to do, which was to nullify the touchdown and penalize Baltimore half the distance to the goal line and Tennessee would have to try again. Jeff happened to be head of the competition committee. But he was also fighting for the playoffs and he said, 'You can't do that, you can't do that.' And I said, 'Coach, you know I can and I have to. You've still got another crack at this.' He was in anguish. He said, 'No, no, we already scored.' Finally he said OK. So I went on the microphone and figured I may as well lay out it out straight to everybody and announce the ruling. The Tennessee crowd can't figure out the delay and it's howling and booing and screaming like something you can't imagine. We were already to make the announcement when Billick yells that he wants to talk to me. He's saying, 'They have to give our guy a chance to get down there on the line of scrimmage.' And I tell him 'Billick, we made the right call and it sticks. I know the cameras are on but if we didn't make that call you lose.'

"He's a very smart guy but he must have figured it was time to protest something. So he says, 'I knew you were right all along.'

"Because the tension was way up and the crowd was waiting, I made a different kind of announcement. I said, 'OK, everybody, with a play of this magnitude I've got to have your attention.' You could hear a pin drop. Then I announced the encroachment, that there was no play and therefore no touchdown and Tennessee had the ball on the one yard line.

The crowd groaned, and they lined up again on the one. Tennessee went for it again and didn't make it. Baltimore won.

"There's a pretty widespread idea among the fans that a team playing at home has one big advantage in the pressure it puts on the officials," Kukar said. "I think that's nonsense. You make the call that's in front of you. The big pressure is to get it right. A lot of times when the game is over, I'll have a little fun with other guys on the officiating team and yell as we're heading for the locker room, 'OK, who won the booing contest today?' In other words who got roasted the most."

Kukar still looks as though he could go three hours with the pros on Sunday afternoon, his winter skiing regimen a carryover from the years when he was subjected to routine fitness checkups by the National Football League, required of all league officials. Those examinations include monitoring body mass and blood pressure and periodic clinical fitness tests. "You've got to be serious about it," he said. "You're not guaranteed that job. You've got to meet standards. You're graded all the time. I grade my own team. If you don't meet those standards, you're bounced." One of the league fitness examiners once asked Kukar how many miles he thought he put in on his most recent game. "About 2½," he guessed.

"Wrong. It was close to 6½."

Every coach in the league, no doubt, has a private rating system of his own and a surplus of candidates for bouncing. The pressures to get it right are tougher on them than the officials. They know if they miss the playoffs for three or four years, or less, they're gone.

But for those guys with the whistles, is it all three hours of high wire tension?

Kukar: "You can't officiate in that league all those years without getting to know a lot of the players, nor would you want to. You learn their personality or character traits, some good, some bad, but mostly you get along pretty well. It was hard not to laugh when Warren Sapp started one of his routines. Warren was a mouth but a lot of fun. We'd get into running conversations. He'd yell, 'Hey, the guy is holding, holding me all the time. Call it!' And you'd tell him, 'Hey, big guy, stop crying. You're too strong for anybody to hold.' But then he'd get playful and tell me, 'I want your cap after the game. You can autograph it.' And I'd tell him 'You can have it if you get to be an official like us.' And he'd giggle and run off some more words."

Imagine Warren Sapp keeping a straight face wearing a whistle and a striped shirt.

Whatever their levels of proficiency, most pro football officials aren't going to attract a high level of adoration from the coaches. With reason. Most of them will louse up a call here and there that can't be rescued by instant replay, and sooner or later those clinkers are going to cost somebody a ball game. A year ago one of the most respected of the NFL referees, Ed Hochuli, blew a call when Denver's Jay Cutler, running to escape blitzers late in a game with San Diego, lost control of the ball. Hochuli ruled that it was an attempted pass. Most of the replay angles established what it was, a fumble, but it wasn't the kind of call Hochuli could change.

Trailing at the time, Denver scored in the final minutes, won the game it would have lost with a correct ruling, and set San Diego off on a losing streak. Hochuli apologized to the San Diego coach, Marv Turner, on the field shortly after the call. It was one of those public embarrassments that are the ultimate horror for the people who blow the whistle and are now paid handsomely to get it right. Hochuli later sent emails trying to explain how it happened and why it happened, and essentially made the already prominent mess a little worse. *Mea culpas* sometimes help, but they don't change the score, and the call cost Ed Hochuli the Super Bowl assignment a few months later. At the league's annual meeting in March of 2009, the rule was changed to make that kind of call reviewable—a sensible decision, though it didn't reverse the score of the Denver game or deliver much comfort to Hochuli.

Kukar retired after 22 years with few regrets and the satisfaction of having worked some of the biggest games of the era, and with some of the most extraordinary personalities ever to play the game.

"I don't know that there will ever be a guy quite like (the late) Walter Payton of the Bears," he said. "I don't say that just because he was one of the great running backs of all time, which he was. But it was his personality that I remember best. He loved the game, the competition. He played every down like it was the end of the world, running hard, running fast and smart. But in a lot of ways he was a kid on the playground. He played a game that was fun for him. He smiled a lot during the game. A guy would knock him down and he'd get up and pat the guy on the back, as though he was saying to the guy, 'Nice tackle. Nice day for football.' And for him it was. In one game, he was under the pile after a run, and as they were unpiling I caught him trying to untie my shoelaces. That kind of guy. You had to love him. Another time he tried to turn my microphone off when I was getting ready to make an announcement. I'd tell him, 'Walter you've got stop doing that stuff.' But I didn't really mean it and he knew it.

"I never saw another guy who played as hard as he did. You'd see him take so many shots, and get up and go back into the huddle and want to carry on the next play. When he died he broke the heart of everybody who ever played with him or against him.

"But I found that the greatest players, almost without exception, were the ones who played the game with respect from start to finish. And they earned the respect of the guys who played against them. Brett Favre is one of them. I think he's the toughest guy I ever saw in football. The blitzers would pound him and sometimes they came in high, but as the years went on you'd see some of the best of the rushers pull up after he released the ball, rather then follow through in a way that might have been legal but also might have hurt Favre. That's the respect they gave him. He never bellyached about a hit that I can remember. You got the same sort of thing from Joe Montana, Jim Kelly, Steve Young, Peyton Manning and other quarterbacks who were true Hall of Famers or will be. It was a pleasure to work with them. Boomer Esiason was a guy who was always a conversationalist. He'd come on the field and say hello and then something like "How are the wife and kids, how's Matthew doing? A real politician, but why not? It didn't save him any sacks but it made life a little easier for people calling the game."

And Bernie Kukar's wife, watching the action at home—naturally she agreed with all of his calls.

"Are you kidding? No way she agreed with all of those calls."

Which ought to comfort Warren Sapp.

4

Bud Grant Rebels Against Stodgy Rules

Down with the fair catch and no-brain extra points? The last-minute kneel? A 5-Star Straight Arrow wants to shake up the game, and make officiating a full-time job along the way.

Picture the Bears against the Packers a few years down the road. The Bears score a touchdown early in the third period, but the Packers are still leading 14-13. And now the cameras reveal animated talk on the Bears' sideline. Millions at home watching television join in a guessing game. What's going on?

It's a dicey scenario. A hard crosswind is blowing. The Bears can choose to run or pass from 2 yards out for two points to take the lead—as they can today—or kicking from nearly 40 yards out for one point to tie the score.

From where? It's the choice they'd have if the National Football League adopts a rules change being pushed by Bud Grant, who is championing a broad menu of revisions he insists pro football needs today to maintain the popularity it has-- and in the process strike a blow for common sense. His hit list of the expendables includes the automatic extra point kick after a touchdown, the fair catch, cheap field goals, the epidemic of penalties on punt and kickoff plays and the time-killing dodge of "taking a knee" to run out the clock while the defense, out of timeouts, watches in stationary misery.

To those changes add full-time officials instead of what Grant considers today's week-end wonders, the officials whose primary work during the week has nothing to do with football.

The coaching decision on the conversion after touchdown today—one point for a kick or two for running or passing from the 2-yard line—is basically no decision. Trying for two points from scrimmage from the 2-yard line has the same appeal for a coach as crawling through a mine field. The extra point kick is a vestigial organ of football dating back 100 years. It once was problematic, when the football was virtually round and was propelled by drop-kickers in baggy pants. With football's evolution and the skills of today's players, it is the equivalent of a 4-inch putt. Counting the 7 yards for the snap of the ball and the 10 yard end zone, the extra point kick today covers 19 or 20 yards. Kids in day care could make the decision, and probably make the kick. Unless he's forced to, the coach is not going run or pass for two from the 2-yard line. So Grant wants to introduce suspense into the conversion. Keep the two-points from scrimmage from the two-yard line as one option, but for the one point placement move the ball upfield to the 20 or better, which means making it close to a 40-yard kick.

"Something like this ought to be in the books," he said, "or a choice close to that. The league mathematicians can figure out the distance it would take for a one-point kick to remain a relatively safe choice—maybe 65 per cent or a little higher—but certainly no sure thing. Then there would be weather conditions to add to the gamble in that decision. Kicking the extra point now is so automatic that it's an invitation to millions of people to head for the refrigerator or the toilet."

Which also means they're likely to miss the beer commercial that comes on the screen just after the ball flies through the goal posts. This is not conjecture. The monitoring meters of the nation's flushing systems reinforce Bud Grant's estimate of what happens in millions of American homes when pro football teams line up for the extra point.

So why not change it? And while we're at it, Grant adds, it might be a good idea to get rid of the fair catch rule and do something about the farce of blocking-in-the-back penalties that have no bearing on a punt or kickoff return. Above all, he insists, do something to upgrade the officiating by making it a full-time job to include weekday shifts at live practice sessions.

"You're never going to convince me that you have to settle for what we have today in officiating in the NFL. The officials are part-time. They're not really coping with the speed of the game, and some of the results of that can be pretty horrendous. That's not going to change much until the league decides to make officiating a full-time profession, the way it is in baseball and basketball."

The picture of Bud Grant as a crusader may clash with his on-the-field image of the immovable gray presence, but success on the field gave him laurels, money and championships. And today that same success gives Grant instant credibility when he insists that pro football can and should be better.

Some of his own coaching heroes were the innovators, chiefly Paul Brown who built the Cleveland Browns and established the benchmarks for successful coaching in the modern era. Grant's own innovations were not spectacular on their face. But

A brief tutorial by Bud Grant

they made a difference in separating him from the herd in the coaching business. That's pretty much the way he saw himself, ahead of the pack not in the headline-catching invention of new playing systems but in the very substantial business of winning football games by creating an edge.

He did it for years. His players needled his backwoods psychology. But he'd been a great athlete and he understood athletes. Sometimes it isn't only money. How the athlete sees himself is important, and accountability is part of being a good athlete. He didn't use the words. But they got the idea, and there was a kind of private professional self-respect with which most of his good teams carried themselves. In the language of the baseball players, most of them played the game right—or they didn't play it. Some of his players had versatilities another coach might not have explored. Some were stars, others relative obscurities who had the attributes to block kicks, an unglamorous craft for sure. Without overdoing it, Grant would make a one-man special team out of an extraordinary football player and competitor like Joey Browner, who was a Pro Bowl strong safety and one of the best athletes Grant ever coached. He was 6-foot-5, powerful and fleet and, as a tackler, devouring. So Grant conscripted him to do extra-duty grunt jobs like covering punts and kickoffs and blocking kicks when he wasn't playing defense. When Browner came back to the bench, wheezing comically and asking for mercy, Grant clapped him on the helmet and said "Joey, you're the best tackler I've got. How can I ignore you?"

Matt Blair was an all-star linebacker. But Grant discovered that his athletic gifts went a lot deeper. At the height of his career, with his size, leaping power and uncommon sense of timing, there was nobody in the league better at blocking kicks. So Matt Blair blocked kicks whenever Grant could get him on the field. So did Tim Baylor and the late Karl Kassulke. In fact, Alan Page, who had an extraordinary sense of anticipation for the snap of the ball, could also be a terror at leaping at precisely the right moment to block an extra point of field goal.

"It was a skill that most fans were totally unaware of," Grant said. "You had guys like Karl Kassulke, who gave everything in his body and mind on every play, and Matt Blair. They had the instincts for it and the motivation. They wanted to do it. They could come off that corner on kicks and throw themselves the moment the ball was kicked. A lot of guys will leap, throw out their arms, and close their eyes. It's a natural reaction. Guys like Matt and Karl and Alan Page kept their eyes open and could actually see the ball coming off the kicker's foot, and throw their hands up into the line of flight. That part of it wasn't instinct. It was playing football at the highest and toughest level."

There were times when an undrafted free agent would ask Grant what he could do to make the team, and the coach would tell him: "Learn to block kicks. You can win a ball game that way."

What he's saying now, away from the coaching lines but as an experienced observer with all of the qualifications, is this:

"Pro football built its large following by being smart in how it negotiated with the television networks and shared the revenue among the clubs. It was smart in the way it conducted the draft, how it worked the schedules and the playoffs and the salary caps. It made itself more exciting with the passing game, brought the kickoff return back into play by moving the kick-off back to the 30-yard line. It developed the instant replay and now cracked down on steroid use and off-field behavior. During this most successful time in history pro football shouldn't forget that we reached that point partly by changing the game with the times. Years ago the NFL pushed the goal posts 10 yards back from the goal line and moved the hash marks. It put in a rule that you couldn't keep bumping the pass receiver 5 yards past the line of scrimmage. It penalized chop blocking, and a lot more.

"But nothing is guaranteed. Pro football should stay ahead of the curve."

Nor did Grant immediately approve of every change that's been brought into the game. Free agency, of course, developed through the courts. But in this and other elements of change, he admits skepticism at the beginning.

"I was like most people when free agency came in," he said. "I worried for a couple of reasons. When I looked at it strictly as a fan would, I thought it would seriously damage the loyalty that football fans give to the team and individual players. You'd have players moving from team to team. That's great for the players, three or four teams bidding for them, although it presents problems for coaches, of course. But we see today that a team can lose a Randy Moss or a Brett Favre or an Edgeron James and the fans may yell, but they pretty much understand that this is now a fact of life. They'll find new stars and stay loyal to the team. It helps, of course, when the team wins.

"I didn't like instant replay when it came in. Most coaches didn't.

It was clumsy and killed time and they didn't know how to manage it. The writers ridiculed it and the crowds and TV audiences scratched their heads and got bored watching the confusion. But they pulled it off the table for three years and fixed it. It's now an important part of the game. It basically works and it's improved the game."

"I think this: we're in the entertainment business in pro football. That's obvious from the ratings, the money, the attendance, and the huge attention pro football gets on television."

"The automatic extra point after a touchdown is an obvious dead spot. They line up for the conversion kick and chances are 99 percent that it's good. One point. Routine. Nothing happens."

"So change it. The two-point run or pass is risky. So put some risk into the extra point kick. Keep the two point conversion from scrimmage at the two-yard line. Give the scoring team the option of kicking for one point from a greater distance than now. Make the break point somewhere that gives the kicking team let's say a 65 percent chance, maybe higher, of getting the one point from further out. That's not as good as 99 ½ per cent that we have today.

"Carry that further. The quickest way to turn off the fans in a professional football game is to reduce it to a battle of field goals, which often equalize each other. I can't argue with coaches who want to get some kind of score when they get close to the end zone. I wasn't shy about it myself. But if you're going to do it with field goals, then why not make the length of the field goal proportionate to the number of points it delivers? Right now you get three points for a field goal no matter where you kick it. You get three points if you kick from 20 yards out and three points if you kick from 50 yards out. Let's change that."

The kicking game receives more emphasis in Canada, as Grant well knows. He played a half dozen positions with the Winnipeg Blue Bombers—after becoming the first player in the National Football League to defy its ownership by playing out his option with the Philadelphia Eagles more than 55 years. He was then offered the head coaching job in Winnipeg, although he had no previous experience as an assistant. Some of the Canadian rules befuddle American fans, and nobody in this country spends much energy trying to figure them out: three downs rather than four, different rules for the passing and kicking games, different rules for substitution and for men-in-motion on offense, and a vast end zone that the receiving team is required to escape on the return or give up a one-point rouge.

One thing the Canadians don't have is a fair catch.

The NFL, Grant believes, needs to do something to enliven the punt return, to eliminate this scenario now familiar to pro football watchers:

The ball is spiraling toward the punt returner. It's a beauty, high enough and gracefully turning over on its nose at the apex of its flight, still a perfect spiral and floating downward toward the return man.

The receiver glances quickly and nervously upfield. The punting team's gunner on the left flank has beaten the defensive double team at the line of scrimmage and is racing downfield. The receiver isn't sure about the gunner on the other side. He lines himself up to catch the descending ball.

And raises his arm.

Fair catch. The oncoming gunner backed off, but not before putting his nose in the face of the return man after he caught the ball in the familiar and snide little act of ex post facto intimidation. So the play was essentially a non-happening. The officials put the ball down on the 15-yard line, after which a beer commercial fills the screen.

The old coach, watching that game on television, groaned. He hates the fair catch. "It's another one of those plays that means nothing. It detracts from what the game is supposed to be all about—fluid action, contact, toughness, suspense, all of that.

"The return man," the interrogator reminded Bud Grant, "had to be thinking how bad it would be if he fumbled near the goal line, and also a little about self-preservation."

The old coach archly thanked the interrogator for reminding him.

"I'm aware of that. But the fair catch play in the NFL is a give-up play, " he says. "In Canada, the return man can't refuse to return the ball. He has to catch it and do something. The ball's always in play. No, he's not going to risk getting slaughtered the moment he catches it. He's got a five-yard safety zone that can't be violated by the kicking team until he catches the ball. That's going to bring more excitement into a routine punt and, incidentally, sometimes give the return team a touchdown where otherwise they'd start from jail."

Grant thinks it's time to reconsider the ten yard penalty for blocking in the back that drives both the coaches and the fans nuts. It can be a brutal game-changer, like the pass interference call. It used to be called clipping, usually associated with blocking below the knees from behind. Now it's any kind of contact from behind, usually in the upper body. There's a good reason for that, to protect a player when he's vulnerable. But now the penalty can be just for pushing and it drives coaches up the wall.

"What hurts is that it's so prevalent," Grant said. "And the reason is that all of the officials are watching the kickoff play. When a play is run from scrimmage the officials have specific areas they police—the linesman for offsides, the back judge for interference-- and they're usually in a position to call only the plays in their area. They can all call a penalty on those wide open kick runbacks, which is why a disproportionate number of those penalties are called. And kick return plays are the ones that are often the most spectacular and go a long way. It's also a penalty that can give you some awful field position.

"Coaches tell their players all the time that if you can see numbers on that jersey, don't block the guy. Don't touch him. But there's a limit on how much time you can spend warning about it. In the end it comes to this: It shouldn't take a lot of smarts to know that if the blocker's back is to you, lay off. Don't touch him."

Most of the kick return team is made up of players who aren't regulars and owe their livelihoods to making it on special teams. For coaches, especially, that makes the penalty especially painful to see an 85-yard runback rubbed out "because (Grant winces here) an official has thrown a flag on a guy who gets into six plays a game and is discovered pushing somebody in the back 40 yards from the football."

In Canada, the kick return man can't down the ball in the end zone and have it brought out to the 20 yard line. He returns it out of the end zone or his team gets nicked one point. "If you concede that the kickoff runback is a truly exciting play, which it is," Grant asked, "then why minimize it as we do now it by letting the guy take a knee in the end zone?

"Make him run it back. I don't care if putting it on the 20 sounds safer than running it out. If he can't or won't run it out, put the ball on his team's 5-yard-line. The game is built on excitement. People will say, pro football is bigger and better now than it has ever been. You know, you actually heard the same kind of talk 30 years ago, and look at the changes that it's made—in some cases changes it's had to make, not only to stay competitive with other sports and entertainment but to keep an edge. I'm saying there are new changes it has to make now."

The clock killing cop-out by a team protecting a lead near the end of the game is one of those schemes that Grant considers a travesty. He didn't say he wouldn't use it if he were coaching today. What he does say is that it shouldn't be available. The scenario is familiar. Team A is leading. It has possession of the ball in the final two minutes. Team B has exhausted its time outs and can't prevent the clock from running. Rather than call a simple play and risk a fumble or interception, the quarterback takes the snap, backs up a yard, and touches the ground with his knee, meaning he's officially down. Folks who genuflect in church know the routine. The clock keeps running. The teams stand around until it's time for the quarterback to do it again. The quarterback does it again and the clock ticks down.

Esthetically, the game ends not with a roar but whisper.

"It's just a lousy way to end a game that's been exciting for 58 minutes," Grant said. "So change it. Put in a rule to make the offense do SOMETHING without putting itself at any big risk. Make the offense run a play that has to get back to the line of scrimmage. It doesn't have to make a gain, just get back to the line of scrimmage. If it doesn't, the clock stops."

So might the hearts of 60,000 people. Make that a few million when you bring in the TV audience. But if the game is supposed to be excitement, the kneel-down is probably not the best billboard for excitement.

Yet for Grant most of the rules irritants pale alongside what he calls the worst threat to law and order in football, which to him is the league policy of maintaining part-time officials.

It's a cause in which Grant probably has millions of converts, especially the ones whose team lost on Sunday. But so far it hasn't seriously dented the aeries of the National Football League high command in New York and is not likely to unless the league is afflicted with a horrendous series of bad calls in high profile games.

Their argument: Officiating in baseball, which Grant uses as a comparison, is unlike football. Baseball is played every day. The umpires, therefore, have to be fulltime professional officials. Pro football plays once a week. Requiring its officials to show up in the middle of the week practices to stay in synch with the speed and tactics of the players is not going to make them better officials.

"They're wrong," Grant says. "If you want to see the results of daily exposure to the game, watch the performance of the first base umpires in baseball day after day. You can argue about balls and strikes by the plate umpire. That's subjective. But the replay camera at first base tells you something pretty remarkable. You get four or five close plays at first almost every game. And it's amazing how often the umpire gets it right. It's one of the bang-bang plays. The throw gets there a split second ahead or behind the runner. Sitting there you make a guess. You're convinced the umpire got it wrong, that the runner was safe. They put on the replay. The umpire was right. The runner was out by a hair. It happens time after time. To me, it's uncanny how many times they're proven right on the replay. And the announcers are often forced to admit it. The fan in the living room guesses on that play. But the umpires see it every day. They know the speed of the game, the relationship of the sound of the ball hitting the first baseman's glove and the runner's foot hitting the bag. They're conditioned to sound and sight working together, based on their experience and watching those plays day after day, year after year."

Grant sees the same kind of value coming to football officials if they're watching football three and four times a week, once during the game but in also in the midweek practices of one of the NFL teams—not, of course, a team whose game they'll be working the following Sunday.

"Right now," he says, "the league protects its officials so much that it's like a cloistered retreat of bishops. And you as a coach can't get into the abbey. You don't know what they're calling. They get graded by the league. The league tells you to call in if you want to know more, but I want to see the grade. It's like working underground. You don't know what they're calling. Ask for an explanation and they give you a bunch of mumbo jumbo. They say 'you can call the league office.' I never called once."

Here is a man clearly generating heat.

"I wouldn't give them the satisfaction of calling."

That is serious heat.

"They'll tell you 'if you've got a complaint, let us hear it.' My answer is you have to get it right the first time. Not next week. The officiating can be significantly improved and made more consistent. And that can be done by the NFL officials coming to practices during the week and watching it full speed. They can do all the film-watching they want on screens as big as the wall. They can slow up the action. They can zoom in the play. They can use all the bright new technology. But none of that is going make them a better official who calls more plays right unless he comes to practice and watches what's happening at full speed."

So how would that work? "Let's say the official is working a game next Sunday between teams A and B. He shows up on Wednesday for the first big practice of the week for Team C. He's not there to get familiar with the personnel and their styles but to stay on top of what professional football teams do, how defensive backs and receivers react on a pass play, the techniques they use, what they do to get an advantage. If it's borderline, what would the official do in an actual game? Those plays are run over and over in practice, and watching them gives the visiting official an idea of what he can anticipate in an actual game, gives him a better feel for it, because the speed of the action that official sees in the practice sessions is a run-up to the speed he'll see and feel on Sunday.

"Don't tell me that doesn't prepare him better than he is now. It means that he is a fulltime employee of the league. He'd be on the payroll, he'd be thinking football all week and he wouldn't be going downtown on Monday morning to be the vice president of a bank. The officials would come from the ranks of younger men who have had some experience with officiating at lower levels, the way it is now. So they could build to a career as a fulltime official in the NFL. A lot of the officials right now are too old and shouldn't be out there. The pay for this kind of professional official would have to be good enough to attract and hold quality people."

NFL officials today are paid partly on the basis of longevity and graded performance. Referees receive considerably more than the others. Depending on performance and years in grade, officials apart from referees can still make anywhere from $40,000 to $80,000. The top shelf officials picked to work playoff and Super Bowl games can earn $100,000 and more.

There are other benefits to the game, Grant contends, that would add to the overall civility of Sunday afternoon on the field.

"The league wants to reduce the pressures on the officials. That's fine, but there are pressures in this game on everybody—the players, the coaches, everybody who's involved in the game because of its huge visibility. If officials are moving around on the practice field, casually encountering the players and coaches, it's bound to make them more human without compromising them. Right now you can't talk to them. They're off limits. You have to have pool reporters going into their dressing room to get information after a controversial call."

Coaches and most players, Grant notes with some sense of mourning, don't breathe such lofty air.

The National Football League is not ready to adopt Grant's

advice on full-time officials. There would be additional expense involved, possibly a union and other issues that would lessen the control the league now has over officiating. None of this surprises Grant nor leaves him penitent.

It also took football awhile, he remembers, to discover the forward pass. Football owes what it has today, he believes, to its pioneers.

Some of Grant's own pioneering as a coach was not widely known because it came in the field of team preparation and it was a little out of the box here and there. But the players eventually bought in. Grant made a virtual cult out of getting his teams ready, both psychologically and strategically, to play and win in ugly weather. He summoned old sourdough logic to keep his teams focused on the job and not on the cold when they played winter football in Minnesota. When the temperature started dropping he'd deliver his annual primer on how to deal with the cold. It got to be fixture in the late season film sessions, happily promoted by veteran players who today after three or four beers at the reunions can recite some of the text verbatim. In their later playing years they virtually demanded to hear it, claiming to be culturally deprived if they didn't. They were basically amused by it—but they got the point.

The story evolved from Grant's years in Canada and actually grew out of the Cold War between the U.S. and Russia. It was the time of the construction of a radar defense network, called the DEW line, to forestall a potential nuclear strike. American workmen installing the equipment, handling bulldozers and other large equipment, initially had a hard time in the severe cold. As part of their indoctrination later, they were told about the Eskimos' ability to work efficiently in super cold conditions, including running the dozers. "That was their habitat," Grant would tell the team, some of them natives of The South and California. "They knew they were going to be cold and there wasn't anything they could do to change the weather, so they did the work and didn't waste a lot of energy being miserable and trying to avoid it. They worked in the cold and did it well and when the job was done they came in out of the cold."

Near the end of his career the players were applauding and yelling "bravo" when Grant finished his story.

But they were aware that they weren't going to get any sideline heaters like the beach crawlers from California on the other bench; which was the crux of Grant's little homily. While the other guys were on the field, freezing and feeling martyred, they were glancing at those roaring heaters on the sideline and thinking how great it would be to get back to them. Grant's Eskimos weren't, and they usually won.

"We always thought the Vikings must be from Mars, the way they played in that icebox," one of the Rams said after a playoff game. "We hated coming to the Met, and we were the last guys to buy into that Eskimo story if Chuck Knox ever tried it on us."

Grant's down-home strategies for preparing his football team and giving it an edge didn't end with the Eskimo saga.

"This league plays into February," he said. "One way or another you're going to play in cold weather. We did it a lot at the old Met stadium, but you still see teams playing practically in blizzards, in Green Bay, Chicago, New England, Denver, New York, Pittsburgh—you can do it in Baltimore. The players used to lobby me for gloves. I told them you can play without gloves, especially handling the ball. Gloves usually don't provide warmth and I told them why. Each finger of the glove is isolated so the fingers can't share body heat with the other fingers, whereas they can when they're not in gloves. When you roll up your fingers or make a fist the fingers warm each other. I told them when they're out in the cold to clap their hands together, it stings. But you do it again, and it stings less. Do it again, and even less. The blood rushes to your hands. Clap your hands and keep doing it, and they start getting warm. Two things happen. You clap your hands, they get warm and you create a little enthusiasm We actually practiced that."

Did the players buy in?

"Some guys did, some didn't."

"What did you tell the guys who didn't."

"I told them they weren't clapping hard enough."

"What happened?

"Most of them clapped harder. Wouldn't you?"

"If I'd been drafted on the sixth round," his visitor said, "I sure as hell would."

But the truth about how Grant managed his football team without going apoplectic or tyrannical went beyond the Old Iron Eyes reputation that followed him. He didn't try very hard to discourage it. He had that persona and he was comfortable with it. But without holding therapy sessions he was serious about the coach-player relationship. And he was also serious about building a kind rough-hewn community and trust among his players around the core of mutual respect.

And he was, for sure, a one and only. His fascination for siphoning out odd patches of information sometimes put him on the edge of caricature. "In training camp in Mankato during the summer I'd listen to the cattle reports on local radio at 6:30 in the morning," he said. "The farmers in southern Minnesota needed to know if it was going be too hot for the cows and they'd have to move them into the shade or get them to water."

Say what?

"I remember setting my radio for this station so I could get up and listen to the cattle report. If the humidity and heat reached a certain number it meant the cows had to have water or shade, which meant the farmers couldn't keep them in pasture all day without food or water. Football players aren't cows. But if the heat and humidity was going to be that high, I wanted to know so I wasn't risking the players' health. On those days I'd tell them to take the pads off and I'd ease up in practice. The players didn't know about the cattle reports, and I was the last guy who was going to tell them, which probably was a good thing because I'll admit it sounds a little kooky—listening to weather advisories to the farmers at 6:30 in the morning."

And making the cattle call you're wake-up alarm. How about giving the game ball to the weather bureau?

But by the way, his teams also won in hot weather.

5

The Media—Football's
Tireless Circus Barker

The country's first laureate of the sports columnists wrote nearly a hundred years ago of the ominous appearance in New York's Polo Grounds of four visitors from the west, dressed in gold and blue.

In Grantland Rice's nimble imagination they evoked a scene from the Bible. They became the Four Horsemen, emerging not from the Apocalypse but from the campus of an obscure Indiana college called Notre Dame. When Grantland Rice wrote, there were no high def screens to compete with his word pictures, no radio to beat him with the news by 24 hours. He was a man of literature and could take his time at the keyboard. He decided to give the Notre Dame backfield—Elmer Layden, Harry Stuhldreyer, Jim Crowley and Don Miller—a name to conjure the dreaded figures out of the scriptures, and that's what they became in perpetuity. A newspaper columnist from New York could do that in the 1920s. It was essentially the beginning of modern sports coverage. Today ESPN would have airlifted the Four Horsemen into the studio at 5 o'clock for a prime-time exclusive.

One day in the early 1980s they put John Madden into a broadcast booth. It took them awhile to get him there because John hated to fly. He arrived by trans-continental bus. But when Madden began telling viewers not only what they were seeing but what made it happen, and doing it like a wise old grampa whose word really WAS the last word, it was the beginning of the televised football-with-tutorials that we know today.

Television football coverage has become so deep and versatile, and the screens so large and revealing that some of the stadium regulars—season ticket buyers for generations—are now beginning to brood over what they're missing. What they're missing, of course, isn't always so glorious. The pre-game buzz on TV is sometimes contrived and frantic, and the happy studio puppet shows at halftime starring defrocked coaches and players are often chaotic. But taken as a whole the Sunday gala of today's television can deliver a show far more alluring, but especially more informing, than what the stadium customers are getting out there in the 30th row for hundreds of bucks more a throw, including parking, mileage, beer and brats. Television can't replace the frenzy that sweeps through the stadium when something big happens and transforms 60,000 people into a hugging and shrieking Community of One. But the people at home are getting far more than comfort and the joys of thrift.

The game their seeing and the action they're getting comes with a clarity on the screen that couldn't have been imagined a few years ago. It comes with a whole rapid fire portfolio of stop-action close ups of the game's pivotal plays—often more of them, in fact, than the referee himself sees under the hood. You have to add one more major component of the show that's unavailable in the 30th row. There, when the home team quarterback blows a pass play, you're going to grumble with the rest. What you don't hear is Phil Simms telling his TV audience that the quarterback didn't screw up when he threw ball two feet over the head of the tight end. The guy who was supposed to catch the ball, Simms says with as much diplomacy as he can, ran the wrong route and it was pretty awful to see.

But rich football owners aren't patsies. So architects of the new stadiums, prodded by club owners, have begun to provide space for giant screens somewhere above the stadium. Assuming they're not knocked down by low-flying blimps, they will give the season ticket-holders the same sight angles and replay sequences now available to the living room watcher. Dallas planned to open its new stadium this year with just such an apparatus. You may not find one immediately at your nearest Best Buy, it is undoubtedly the Sky Screen of the future. The owners of other stadiums are likely to follow Dallas's lead, if they can get appropriate clearance from the local air traffic control.

So the stadium audience will soon be getting a monster view of the play it just saw with the now grossly inadequate naked eye. One thing the stadium crowd will still lack is the voice of experience in the broadcast booth, telling them WHY it happened.

Such technical advances in TV and on the internet are hardly the worst new challenges to the newspapers that once dominated sports coverage. Dwindling revenue and increasing debt have driven once-powerful publishing families into fire sales to Wall Street equity firms. Yet the sports pages of the daily papers have not been abandoned entirely by the public. On Monday mornings millions of Americans still reach for them to absorb the story and the post-mortems of the locker room. If their team won, football nerds have been known to stand in pajamas on the doorstep before dawn waiting the arrival of the delivery van. Why? Gloating is best enjoyed when it's stretched out—first the broadcast itself, then the highlight reels on TV, the internet, then the morning newspaper accounts. If the team lost, demoralized fans may stay in bed and let the obituaries of the game sit on the doorstep soaking up the rain.

On radio and TV, of course, it's round the clock, and anybody who watched the game can get into the post-game autopsies. Fans can do it with call-ins to radio and TV, on the web and with their blogging energies. The writers of the newspaper's game stories are hardly robots and stenographers. They're going to be making their own judgments of the strategies and the quarterback's rag arm along with the reportage. In fact in today's journalism it's almost required for credibility.

So when the game is over the deluge of talk and comment begins and we hear the voices of kangaroo judgment from anybody with a cell phone handy. It's a carnival on radio and television, reminding us that this is well and truly the information age. Laws of libel and slander are not seriously recognized in the cacophony. All of the mainstream media websites today invite viewer comments, in fact plead for them. Feedback measures the reach and popularity of the website, which tells advertisers where to go with their dollars. It's why the TV news cables poll the viewers ad nauseam for their opinions. Newspapers do the same thing in their struggle to hang on to readership.

Bloggers on the internet can be both unstoppable and ungovernable, with an open invitation to be as smart, vulgar, funny, arrogant or as literate as they want. Increasingly, though, the more thoughtful writing in the blogosphere is finding its way into newsprint.

This can be tiring but it also can be a welcome additive to a newspaper's coverage, depending on how it's managed. Democracy progresses by unpredictable swerves and lurches. It's basically a measure of the times, which imposes more requirements along with more resources for today's journalists. And that includes, of course, the sports writer, who is committed to both his newspaper's print and internet, and sometimes it's a 15-hour carousel.

This is how coverage runs today inevitably. Is it better coverage than 30 years ago?

In some ways it emphatically is. It's breezier, more adept in the language of the game, and probably better informed in the strategies of the game. Is it as humane?

Not likely. Is it required to be more humane?

No, it's not.

So is it fair? That depends on the writers and editors, and the reader's perception. Also the coaches. In 2007, Tom Coughlin of the Giants took an almost weekly lacing from the game reporters of the prestigious *New York Times* and, of course, the tabloids. They picked his bones on his game management and sniffed at his glowering attitude. His relations with the players were probed and prosecuted. He was depicted as a man two months away from being fired, losing control and disliked. Nothing much about him had changed since the beginning of the season.

Two months later his team won the Super Bowl, reminding us that sometimes, and often, the coaches have more guts than their critics.

In today's news reporting you will read what happened, what might have happened and what should have happened. For the columnist there are looser boundaries now between literate and informed commentary, smug commentary and actual defamation. The inevitable expansion of media coverage to include bloggers and call-in wonks has opened the fraternity to a wide array of wise guys, rascals and imposters. But it also has uncovered some pretty colorful insight. And the popularity of some of the amateurs on the internet has stirred the newspapers' editors to recognize this expanding Fifth Estate by opening their pages to it.

The truth is that in today's media market, ratings and hits matter everywhere.

Which means the professional reporters and commentators today in print and broadcast can't get by without a true insider's knowledge of the sport they're covering. The audiences are more aware and the competition is everywhere. Because it is, the actual reportage in print journalism today can be more incisive and is better informed than it was years ago, when the pace was calmer and sanity at least had a chance in defining the place of athletics in American society.

Television and the internet have pretty much altered the rules of engagement in the cross-cultures of journalism in sports. The successful local columnists today usually find their way to television and radio, partly because the local television stations have a vested interest in the success of the teams they air, making them de facto partners. So they're not going to do a whole lot of off-with-their-heads commentary about their clients. It means the newspaper writer or columnist with an established audience can bring range and a little more credibility to their coverage. But television can also make life miserable for the print journalist. ESPN's reach and the alliances it forms with some of the headline players sometimes gives it more reliable access to those players than the beat reporter has.

Older readers sometimes complain about what they call attack journalism. It can be abrasive and cruel. Some of its practitioners will admit in their private confessionals that's its better when the locals lose, which makes it easier to write that way. Almost nobody wants to write continuing fluff to feed the public's glorification of its redeemed heroes. It's boring and professionally unrewarding. But not many sports columnists can get by with daily ripping and hell-raising, which eventually will wear out normal readers who don't need daily doses of sadism to add to their troubles with bills. One thing the ripsmith never wants to do when he (or she) unleashes his (or her) thunderbolts is to consider the outside possibility that there might be another side to the story.

But in general the sports commentary you get in today's newspaper is likely to be more thoughtful and, if not that, certainly more informed than most of what you see or hear on the call-in radio show or the manic television studio shows of contrived baiting and mugging among the studio hosts. It should be said that Bob Costas' weekly interviews and commentary on radio have represented some of the very best in broadcast journalism, or any journalism. Most of the straight writing in today's newspaper, for all of its dwindling resources, performs the required service of telling the reader what happened and, with some style and buoyancy, taking the reader inside the establishment. If the quarterback's lousy throws cost the game, it can be said, and usually is, without making him a misfit. You can express your shrewd judgments and still leave open the outside chance that (a) you may be wrong or (b) the victim is a decent human being who doesn't belch at weddings and really does know something about playing the game. The Red Smiths and Dick Cullums of the journalism of other eras wrote well and convincingly, could fix blame without maligning the player, kept their big audiences and did it for decades.

John Madden didn't write much but he did talk, and the viewer was better for it, not only better schooled but probably relieved knowing that the running back fumbled the ball not because he forgot the snap count but because the quarterback's handoff practically gave him a hernia.

In today's football coverage, it's the broadcast analyst who has the huge audiences and in this John Madden, now retired, was the godfather of the breed. Madden offered his asides, volunteered or prompted by Al Michaels, in a bulky and unpretentious way that was generally kind but also impatient with mediocrity. He delivered criticism neutrally but convincingly. He gave the impression of being an ultimate authority, professional but willing to lay down a judgment when the audience needed to know that what it just saw was a miserable attempt by the fullback to cut off the pass rusher.

Madden has had his detractors over the years, for being heavy-handed and rumbling, but mostly for being old and gruff. But his commentary established the gold standard for informed critique in the early years of professional analysis on TV. Along the way some viewers simply got tired of hearing his voice, but the conversational shorthand of his analysis never irritated me. Madden in the broadcast booth gave me an extra invitation to the game, whether it was one of no special significance or the Super Bowl.

It was rarely an insignificant game. The networks don't assign their most visible assets to the meatball games. He was good not because he knows the game utterly as a Super Bowl-winning coach. They all know the game utterly. Bill Parcells was for several years the best coach in football. In the years when he did the booth analysis he gave you most of the inside football you need, and he was good. But Parcells was tart and cryptic and careful not to betray the tough love he felt for the game and some of the players in it. You weren't going to get both his mind and his glands into the game when he was in the booth.

The broadcast evolution also has had the effect of demanding from the play-by-play announcer a knowledge of the game that is very close to the analyst's himself. So you had the teaming of Madden with Al Michaels, of Troy Aikman with Joe Buck, with the mutual respect that in a partnership like this is vital.

For much of the viewing public, all of this adds up to a spontaneous education into what used to be the mysteries of the game. During the early days of telecast football we watched it in black and white on our screens. We listened to the announcer in the booth and followed the action by means of two or three cameras at the disposal of the televising station or network. Halftime entertainment often consisted of a marching band. Later a football expert was added to the show. He could take the viewer inside the game, explain the formation, point out that the offense had to have seven men on the line of scrimmage, clarify what the quarterback was doing with his hut-huts behind the center and why the defense was shifting before the snap of the ball.

It was a beginning. In those years some of the announcing was inadequate to the opportunities and challenges that TV brought to football. A lot of the play by play announcers were not prepared and failed to convey the tension and drama at the core of the game. But there were others who pioneered in the combination of theater and expertise that we commonly see and hear today. One of them was the late Ray Scott, who primarily did the Packer games for the network. He had a commanding voice and a working savvy of the game's strategies, and he also recognized that you don't call a football game on television the way they once did and still have to do it on radio, which is to create a picture: "Jones drops back to pass, he has time, the rush is slow getting to him, he throws....and the ball sails over Avogadro's head."

Scott understood that there was no need for a TV announcer to tell viewers what they could already see. Identify the central figures in the play. When the play's in progress, give the audience what it needs but don't be a distraction.

So Jim Ringo would snap the ball to Bart Starr, who turned and handed it to the running back, and Scott would say "This....is Hornung" as Paul Hornung ran a sweep into your living room. Scott introduced the running back, almost presented him, and the play was on. The technique was simple, terse and dramatic.

Scott had the insider's knowledge of the game, but probably not at the level of today's best announcers, among them Michaels and Buck. The voice of wisdom at their side can quickly and confidently tell you why the middle linebacker bit on the fake screen pass. Madden was the pioneer and franchise holder in analysis without gobbledygook. Collinsworth, Aikman, Dan Diersdorf, Phil Simms and others also bring a dimension to the TV presentation that explains the play, the game, the technique, tactics and the euphoria and pain that we see on the field, all of which has broadened the experience for the viewer. During the black and white era the game had drama. Today viewers seem directly involved because they not only feel the tension, see the action but are on the inside of the strategy.

Collinsworth is the next Madden in the NBC pairings. He is a former wide receiver with a quick and discerning mind, clear in his observations and his argument. He has no trouble being judgmental and, as needed, he can be a prosecutor. In addition, not many analysts work harder at the job. Mike Tirico, Tony Kornheiser and Ron Jaworski were fun but sometimes presented a challenge. Three's a crowd in any booth and it's often hard to know who was masterminding the show unless the camera comes into the booth. Kornheiser's strengths were in his exquisite pre-game essays, not his comedy. He has now been replaced by Jon Gruden, the former coach. Tirico is a sound professional and gives you a play by play that reflects the tension of the game. Jaws Jaworski is a one-time star quarterback with a trigger mind for the game's offense, a friendly and happy guy with the ability to demystify the technical intricacies of playing quarterback in the NFL. He may actually be the most purely informative of all the commentators. The problem there is three in a booth, which can be suffocating to the viewer when they bring in a network guest to hype his latest film.

But I remember Madden doing a Minnesota-Detroit game. His off-camera observations put you into the huddle and on the line of scrimmage more credibly and more intimately than anybody doing the analysis gig. When Madden did the game you could hear the grunts from those people and feel their sweat. The fact that some of the grunts came from Madden was simply giving you a football man being a football man. So he would ignore the usual niceties and blurt impatiently as the Lions let time bleed off the clock with two time-outs left in the half: "That was stupid clock management by the Lions." Eventually he was actually yelling, personally enraged by this breach of professionalism by the Lions. "It just wasn't very good. What am I talking about, 'not very—? It was absolutely stupid."

I liked that from Madden because it reinforced my own bafflement in the face of what the Lions were doing or not doing. At unpredictable moments Madden would wander back to his coaching years to flesh out the game. He knew what worries the linemen, what arouses them emotionally and why the Lions' defensive scheme is an invitation to suicide. That and what the little defensive backs are thinking when one of those ball-carrying heavyweights—remember Christian Okoye, the Nigerian Nightmare—comes pounding into the secondary with his 250 or 260 pounds and his knees high: "I tell you you're not going to find a whole lot of people who want to get in front of this guy when he comes out of that line," John was saying.

Is that the way it is out there? Fear, even in the insides of professional football players? "The little defensive backs," the runaway tanks like Okoye and Mike Alstott and now the Giants' Brandon Jacobs would tell you, "they'll tackle you. But they'd rather not."

On that day Madden remarked that he didn't think the Vikings had the goods to go deep into the playoffs. Which they didn't. That view was tempered by the sight of Randy Moss gliding through the Detroit secondary after deeking the Lions cornerback and then racing into the end zone on the end of a long pass. With Moss in his early days, Madden never bothered with professional restraint. "Randy Moss," he said, "is a super, super football player. Robert Bailey (a Lions' defensive back) might want to know what happened to the help he was supposed to get from the safety. If he was supposed to, it didn't happen. There is nobody in football who can cover Randy Moss one-on-one."

Moss left the Vikings a couple of years later, disturbed by a half a dozen irritations, including the absence of a quarterback with the wisdom to throw the ball to Randy Moss on every play. He was a disruption and needed to go but he suffered miserably in Oakland before being resuscitated by Tom Brady and Bill Belichick in New England. There is no record that Madden has ever changed his estimate of Moss' brilliance as a receiver.

The message there is that sometimes all the most gifted athletes need is somebody in the game to showcase their brilliance—and somebody creditable enough in the booth to identify it.

6

Be Kind to Nostalgia,
Remember McElhenny and Dutch

There are people in this country half-convinced that pro football today is the promotional invention of the makers of Viagra, the peddlers of Foot-Long Subways, and the survivors of Demolition Derby who are now trying to sell cars on television by smashing them into firewalls.

Millions of people who watch the pro football on television seriously confess addiction. In their calmer moments they will admit it's a buzz watching millionaires beating the hell out of each other.

Somewhere in there, normalcy counterattacks. The truth is that most people who watch pro football do it on the day or night of the game and then rejoin the real world of bills, family, church and recessions.

But for the truly committed, televised pro football is the candy store that never goes sour. For them, pro football is endless and virtually a condition of life. It's incessant and unapologetic. It's there in the run-ups to the player draft in spring and in those awesome moments when the first round choices are announced in an atmosphere soaked with tension. It is less a draft than a coronation.

Such obsessive interest, and the multi-culture merchandising that goes along with it, is something that ancients among us would never have imagined 40 years ago. And it can be traced to the moment more than 40 years ago when young Pete Rozelle, the newly-installed NFL

Fran Tarkenton (center) and teammates Ron Vanderkelen (11) and John McCormick (15) strike a publicity pose in the Vikings' training camp in 1962.

commissioner, went to the television executives and said, "I think you might want to seriously consider what you can make out of pro football."

I confess to being a registered member of the ancients. Professional football was one of my beats when Francis Tarkenton signed a contract for the cosmic sum of $12,500 to quarterback the Minnesota Vikings in their first year of competition. In 1961 almost anyone could walk on for a tryout. In fact, an unemployed butcher from Muskegon in Michigan did. It was a time when success in Norm Van Brocklin's two-a day survival clinics wasn't measured by promotion to the first team but by the number of players still standing at the finish. At least one of the Dutchman's free agents barely made it, an overweight tackle who had run through the agility ropes a half dozen times, listing badly on the last few runs. In those years weight lifting and year-round conditioning were not part of the preparation. Almost nobody lifted weights or ran miles. Most of them were working in odd jobs during the winter to pay for groceries. In summer camp they ran the ropes, again and again, and then ran more ropes. Or they hammered the blocking sleds.

On this day in the Viking training camp in Bemidji, the candidate tackle was determined but fading fast. When the drill was over he sank on the grass, gasping. The trainer, Fred Zamberletti, was at his side in a flash and did all the required tests and procedures. The guy was going to survive. All of his vital signs were good and getting better. Fred offered comforting words. The tackle was not convinced and his eyes were large. "What can I do for you?" Fred asked. "Man," he said, "take me to the church. I think I'm gonna die."

After getting the medical report, Van Brocklin shifted the young man's destination from the church to the airport, ending his professional career at one day.

It might have been a rare act of kindness. The next day Van Brocklin scrimmaged not once but twice and had half the team diving into the nearby lake for recovery.

Some of us were passable romanticists in those years. The arrival of major league football in the Twin Cities didn't overwhelm the cities, but it was a tantalizing turn of events and Norm Van Brocklin was at the center of it. After 12 years as a superstar quarterback with the Los Angeles Rams and Philadelphia Eagles, he retired to begin a new career as Coach Genghis Khan of the of the Vikings' new NFL franchise. To the practice field in the northwoods of Bemidji he brought a brilliant mind, an owly disposition and a take-no-prisoners mentality.

The lore began about then. Hordes of today's Viking followers would be surprised to learn that the team originally was in the hands of a sulphurous coach who once threatened to throw one of his line-men off the plane at the impractical altitude of 25,000 feet. Scarcely a Viking fan today remembers that the first Minnesota Vikings were a composite of brooding malcontents and flotsam rescued from the rest of the National Football League, joined on the opening day of practice by a busload of unwary rookies taken in the draft. The sagas of those early years just don't deserve oblivion.

There were no player associations then. What Van Brocklin's ath-letes really needed was a chaplain. His camps in the pine groves were often compared with the old French exile prison camps on Devil's Island, from which there was no escape. But a week into practice the first year, one of the free agents reported to his assistant coach that his room-mate was gone.

Norm Van Brocklin

"Did he say anything about why, some emergency or something?" the coach asked.

"No. But he left a note."

"Well?"

"It said 'Goodbye, roomie, I'm outa here. I choose life.'"

Inevitably, some of the players schemed relief from the daily exhaustion. There were curfews, of course. But fully aware of Van Brocklin's Captain Bligh reputation, the veteran inmates schemed escape on the nights when it looked safe for some serious hell-raising.

Bemidji was and is a northwoods lumbering town. It is also the home of an attractive college, where the Vikings trained for the first six years. From his long-time observations in the field of boy-girl phe-nomena, Van Brocklin saw something unmistakably dangerous about dumping 80 football players into a nest of 500 coeds, to say nothing of the young working women around town and in the more remote reaches of Turtle River, Bagley, Blackduck and other small towns. He made an announcement early during the first camp. It was a model of clarity. All that was missing was the sound of a judge's gavel.

Van Brocklin said: "There will be no fraternizing. Period. By fraternizing I mean dating, dancing or invitations to look at your clippings. I'm not doing this for your protection or their protection. I'm doing this for the simple and selfish protection of the Minnesota Vikings.

"We'll have some kind of rest leave for anybody who shows signs of cabin fever here in the woods. I repeat. There WILL BE NO FRATERNIZING. We are not going to fine you. We are not going to suspend you. We are just going to put your butt on the next plane out of town."

The fact that the next plane out of Bemidji in those years was a DC-3 probably added an extra touch of angst in the hearts of Van Brocklin's warriors.

In the dormitory rooms where the players were housed, Van Brocklin's sermon was met with no surprise but also, among the older players, with no special terror. After two or three weeks in camp a sizable number of the athletes reasoned that there were worse fates than getting kicked off Van Brocklin's football team. In the 1960s, humanitarian behavior by NFL coaches was not part of the contract and there were no platoons of assistant coaches or free lance shrinks to offer consolation. Van Brocklin's edict was rigidly observed on campus. But it could be outflanked at a hilltop 3.2 beer joint called, of all things, The Dutchess. Except for the bowling alley near the college where the players consumed vats of beer after practice in 90 degree heat, The Dutchess was the only place in town where they could congregate without drawing a $100 fine from Van Brocklin or cold stares from the town's mothers.

The Dutchess resembled a converted stockade that had survived the Chippewa wars. On a windless day it was touched by colliding aromas reminiscent of the town zoo. As a convenience the men's biff had been moved to the parking lot bushes. The Dutchess was the players' dance hall, wailing wall, drinking trough and confessional. Its ownership was never clearly established. But there had to be an awful lot of charity in the hearts of the local gendarmes to keep it open. At times when complaints about wild parties couldn't be ignored without the threat of a legislative hearing, the local enforcers would stage a combined operation. It was officially classified as a raid but it was actually an extension of the social hour.

The astonishing part of all this is that less than two months later, the Minnesota Vikings, a team cobbled from a deportation list of washouts and football nomads, joined by a handful of quality rookies like Fran Tarkenton and Tommy Mason, would beat the Chicago Bears by three touchdowns in its first game as a registered football team.

One credible explanation was that playing an honest-to-God football game was a relief after six weeks in Bemidji.

The survivors of Van Brocklin's training camps came to acquire the unbreakable bond of men who have shared the rack. It was left for the last Sunday of camp, however, for Van Brocklin to deliver his final blow of revenge against the misguided rebels who violated his curfew rules. The body count at the midnight curfew of the final Saturday night turned up three absentees—two of the wiliest veterans, Charlie Sumner and Bill Bishop, and a rookie fullback, Raymond Hayes.

At 8 a.m. Sunday Van Brocklin stalked into the dormitory room of the equipment manager, Jimmy Eason, a little guy much loved by the players and a war hero who had lost a leg in World War II. Along with the rest, Van Brocklin loved Eason, but this was another kind of war and he grabbed the foot of Eason's cot and spilled the startled little man on the floor.

"Wassa matter," Eason said. "It's Sunday. We don't have to eat breakfast."

"We're doing an extra workout this morning," Van Brocklin said. "Get down to the dressing room." Eason had a running start on a hangover himself. Noticing Van Brocklin's red-streaked eyes and rising belligerence, Eason figured out quickly that the Dutchman didn't need any more conversation. Sumner, Bishop and Hayes appeared at

9 a.m. Eason issued the full battle gear—helmets, shoulder pads, blocking pads, the works. From the training room they walked the quarter of a mile to the practice field. There was a foreboding in their hearts and a funereal pace in their tread. Van Brocklin was waiting for them in the middle of the field. The August sun was rising in the cloudless sky, pouring nearly 90 degree heat on the hardening field. Birds fluttered in the nearby oaks and the other innocent sounds of Sunday morning in the pines played lightly on the scene.

Another day it might have been a time for poets, but Keats never had to play against Big Daddy Lipscomb and Geno Marchetti of the Baltimore Colts in an exhibition six days later.

Van Brocklin stopped the approaching trio at the goal line.

"All right," he said. "I want you to roll end over end down the field to the other goal line."

They rolled to the other goal line.

"All right," he said, "I want you to roll back to the other goal line."

They rolled to the other goal line.

They rolled back and forth, 100 yards at a time. And then they leap-frogged and somersaulted. Even when performed by a healthy man, these are unnatural acrobatics that can cause upheavals in the abdominal tracts. Sumner, Hayes and Bishop were already carrying the handicap of dark spots in the eyes and queasy innards. After an hour they pleaded for a time out. Van Brocklin was untouched. Mercy wasn't in the play book. They were reeling and approaching a 4-G blackout condition.

The temperature mounted past 90. In scores of dormitory windows and from behind oak trees, awed teammates viewed the endless and wobbly gymnastics. Two of them rented a rowboat for a closer vantage point from the bay of Lake Bemidji and nearly drowned when Van Brocklin turned suddenly as they neared shore. The movement panicked the boaters and the boat capsized.

On the field, the rollers were getting sick. And the sicker they got the more penitent they became. "Coach," one of them said, "take five hundred bucks outa my pay but don't make me roll down that field one more friggin' time."

"Roll down that field one more friggin' time," Van Brocklin said.

With the hour approaching 11, Van Brocklin picked his way through the messy field and left the three reeling acrobats semi-conscious at the goal line.

But they struggled to their feet and made their way toward Eason's training room. Exhausted in the middle of the street, Hayes stopped to suck in air. This was awkward because a semi-trailer was coming down the street after making a quick turn. The driver stopped, uncertain about his truck's chances in a collision. Hayes started to wave his thanks but the driver had heard about Van Brocklin and got out of there in a hurry. Two of the players eventually made it non-stop but Bishop sank onto a curb halfway to the dressing room. He remained there motionless for nearly 15 minutes and, unbeknownst to him, became the subject of a passing art class.

There were no curfew violations in Bemidji that night.

But it was a feast for the few embattled souls covering the team. Essentially there were just two of us, the beat writers for the Minneapolis and St. Paul newspapers. Nothing then approximated the posses and paparazzi that are organized to report on the pro football teams today—the print writers, the TV reporters and camera people, aces from the TV networks, magazine writers and more.

M y buddy of the print press in those days was the late and highly affable Roger Rosenblum of the *St. Paul Dispatch* and *Pioneer Press*, a beefy lover of the opera and the arts whose expansive tastes included good gin and Wellington steaks. One year before a Viking-Lions game in Detroit we shared a table with a reporter from one of the New York dailies. Herb Carneal, the much-venerated baseball announcer who was then also doing television football, was in the party, along with the Vikings' PR director, John Thompson, and a few others. There was no question in the minds of any of the regulars at the table that Roger was a heroic eater. We so advised the New York visitor, who seemed unimpressed early. He said he had seen some of the outstanding gourmands on Broadway. Roger began with a tuna fish salad and then knocked down a 16-ounce steak with relative ease, along with a dozen blue points and a small mountain of cheese-laced mashed potatoes, plus a pair of martinis. Now well and truly under-way, he ordered a smaller steak, pausing briefly to dab his bread roll in the gravy on a nearby plate. This surprised Carneal, who was under the assumption that the plate was his, which it was. After he cast a look of genial surprise at Roger, Rosenblum smiled an apology and finished the second steak in the midst of a second round of blue points.

There was a mild stir at the table and the visiting New Yorker excused himself for a few minutes. He went to a nearby phone and di-aled his favorite restaurateur in New York, the celebrated Toots Shor, who served Hollywood stars and political elite, athletic headliners and flocks of millionaires. We overhead part of the conversation. "Shor," he said. "I can't believe this. I've seen world class eaters. I once shared a table with Minnesota Fats. But this guy is awesome. He's in another league. He belongs in the Olympics."

After which Roger tastefully ordered another helping of quiche.

There were no order-of-battle rules about how you covered a pro football team in those days. The professional detachment required to-day was not entirely possible or wholly workable in those years. You needed to avoid being co-opted by the club or some of its personali-ties, of course. You had to maintain an independence and some level of honor about what you wrote and what you didn't, because the locker room was pretty much privileged territory although perfect for the more formal interview that could be printed. I strolled freely every day through the Viking locker room, absorbing the usual harpoons, and hearing but trying to ignore conversation not intended to be re-ported. You would witness but not report the odd locker room fight between Paul Dickson and Steve Stonebreaker—until it was more or less history. Jim Marshall, the venturesome defensive end, joined one of my snowmobile runs to the Beartooth Pass in the western moun-tains one year, and we nearly died together in a ground blizzard. You could have that kind of relationship in those years without giving up the hard core of professional independence.

The locker room dialogue you left pretty much alone, but it was okay to hear George Shaw, the veteran quarterback, remembering a battle-hungry lineman with the Baltimore Colts. "A guy who was really dedicated to football," Shaw told a locker mate, "was our center, Dick Syzmanski. He was bachelor then. Dick told me he would lie awake nights trying to figure out new ways to hit people."

This drew a pained reflection from one of the listeners, Hugh McElhenny, the great running back of that era.

"Me," McElhenny said, "I used to lie awake nights trying to figure out new ways to not to get hit."

Hugh McElhenny. The nostalgist who is now conditioned to the marvels of pro football in the 21st Century, has to pause remembering a special quality Hugh McElhenny gave to the game. When McElhenny ran it was with a kind of fluid creativity in full stride not quite duplicated by any of the great runners more familiar to the crowds of today. He didn't have the power-plus-speed of Eric Dickerson or the raw force and will of Jim Brown or the acrobatics of Barry Sanders or the indomitability of Walter Payton. He was Hugh McElhenny, the best runner of his generation, nine years with the San Francisco 49ers, winding down when he came to the Minnesota Vikings for two years in 1961 and '62. But even that late in his career, when he arrived he was introduced to the squad by Van Brocklin as "The King of the Half-backs," bronzed, curious, and vaguely out of place among the outcasts and rookies with whom he played in his approaching valedictory.

McElhenny was simply one of those irreplaceables. He met the classic definitions of a great halfback as it was defined in those years. His movements were sinuous and intuitive. He ran with grace and speed, with changes of direction and tempo, but always under control. He brought to the field and its homicidal tacklers what the matador brings to the bull ring—the same finesse, measured doses of bravado, and, when it was needed, nerve. McElhenny was a likable guy with a face usually lit by an inviting grin and darkened by the sun of the California beaches. He carried no special airs about being a football star. When he got to Minnesota he was filling out his last years as a

Future Hall of Famer Hugh McElhenny swings left (photo 1) to begin his classic run against the 49ers, first eluding Leo Nomellini (73) who was also destined for the Hall of Fame, then (photo 2) Dave Baker.

professional football player, an aging virtuoso athlete who had a balanced view of the world but was hardly immune to the usefulness of the dollar bill. In Seattle, where he played his final two seasons at the University of Washington, they still remember McElhenny's smiling observation that he had to take a pay cut to go from collegiate football into the NFL. But he wasn't a wise guy and he ran with a grace, speed and bravura that years later brought him into the NFL's Hall of Fame.

I wrote later of a moment at the now deceased Metropolitan Stadium nearly 50 years ago when Hugh McElhenny re-ignited all of the electricity that accompanied a classic McElhenny run. This one—perhaps not so coincidentally—came against the 49ers who had abandoned him. It gave you the fluid gymnastics of the professional open-field runner. None of it was for show. His moves always had meaning—a limp leg here, a dipped shoulder there. The football fan who understood the nuances of his craft prized Hugh McElhenny almost above all other great football players in that era. He appealed to the aficionado's admiration of style wedded to speed. His kind of football theater took him a little beyond the spectator's emotional partisanship. He might have beaten you but he rarely wounded you. The fan whose team lost to the power of the Packers or the speed of the Cowboys might have found scapegoats and villains in his own

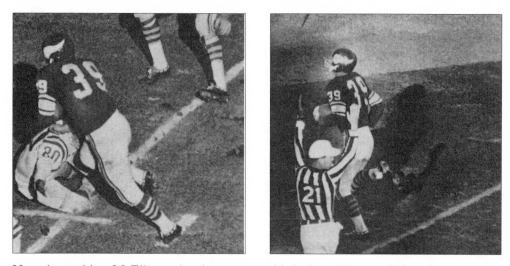

Near the goal line McElhenny breaks an arm tackle by Jerry Mertens (80) and then bursts into the end zone. (Photos courtesy the *Minneapolis Star Tribune*.)

ranks, but losing to McElhenny rarely left him with any hostility. And when he raced into the end zone he did not evoke the instant thunder that follows a spectacular catch. The reaction was closer to the bravo applause of the concert hall. The greatest McElhenny plays were pure concert, and it was not until they were over that he would allow himself that reflexive showmanship to which the great ones are entitled—a high stride into the end zone with his head thrown back.

His last such performance was on a sunny October day at the Met, when he reached back into his prime for a valedictory run, as if to place his unique signature at the end of a grand career. He made other runs in his last years and scored again, but against the 49ers on that day—

McElhenny swung to the left behind two pulling guards, dipped back slightly and started to turn the edge. He needed only 32 yards. But the guards disappeared somewhere around the line of scrimmage. McElhenny ducked away from the cornerback and slipped the outside linebacker. He veered toward the center of the field. Linemen hit him at the hips and shoulders but they never hit him hard. He was always a half step away from the crunching shoulder or somebody's tripping hand. He dodged Matt Hazeltine, who ironically was his insurance broker in San Francisco. He was now at the 20 and he strait-armed the safety. Even while he was in full stride, the spectator's gaze had to fall behind him to scan a remarkable graveyard of sprawled bodies. By actual count on film, seven players had open shots at him during that run, but none of them caught more than a swatch of nylon or a vanishing pad. He was in high stride now, swinging toward the goal line, and there was Matt Hazeltine—again. McElhenny pulled his shoulder in and Hazeltine flew by him harmlessly.

With the end zone underfoot, McElhenny raised his knees a little and pranced in, handed the ball to the official and trotted to the Viking bench. There, the Vikings' first round draft choice, Tommy Mason, also a running back, told a teammate: "I wanted to ask him for his autograph on the spot."

Van Brocklin clasped his hand and might have been telling an audience new to the pro game: "This is the NFL at it's best."

It was almost exactly what the Chicago football writers said, in fact, when they presented McElhenny with a plaque 10 minutes before the Bears-Vikings final game of the season.

It read: "Wouldn't football be a beautiful game if everybody played it like Hugh McElhenny?"

Fifteen minutes later Hugh McElhenny ran back a punt 81 yards for a touchdown.

He was not an especially heroic man, although he had nerve enough when he needed it. He didn't function well when injured and he never pretended anything different. He didn't dog it in practice, but he was also abundantly aware that he didn't sell any tickets with practice performances. In a way he was the last issue of a breed, the halfbacks who saw the field as tapestry and read the texture on the fly. A McElhenny run might turn a five-yard sweep into an 80-yard frolic. In later years, as defensive linemen and linebackers became quicker and more aggressive in pursuit, his game of parry and thrust rounding the corner had to change.

"Years ago, if you turned the corner you only had a couple of guys to beat. By the time I finished playing ball it wasn't the linebackers in front of you who were breaking up the long run, it was the guys coming all the way from the other side, the ones nobody blocked because they weren't supposed to be in the play. It was a tough combination for a runner as he got older: the linemen were getting bigger and faster and they were in great shape, which tended to make life hazardous for guys like me.

"But I loved it."

And so the new great runners became the ones who approached McElhenny's speed but had more natural power to handle the encroaching musclemen—Jim Brown and Gale Sayers and Calvin Hill, and then O. J. Simpson and Eric Dickerson, Emmit Smith and even Walter Payton with his surprising strength to complement his speed and dexterity.

But McElhenny is the runner the ancients like me remember with a special kind of wistfulness, because he seemed to be carrying some sort of secret—how to survive the onrushing elephants—and to do it in style.

Which he did, on almost every carry. His best are still engraved in my mind of anyone who saw him run.

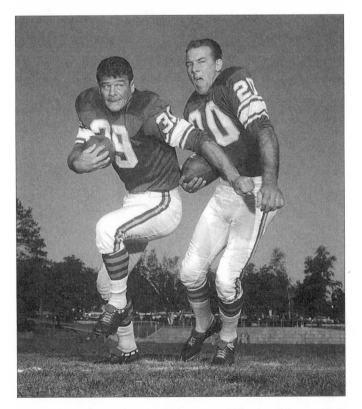

Backfield tandem Hugh McElhenny and Tommy Mason, 1962

7

The Game of Sacks and Hula Dances

The man who handles the classics counter at a Minneapolis music store, John Swann, was a football watcher for years. During the 2008 season one of his football-minded customers asked whether he was going to take in the telecast of the NFL's showpiece game of the week between the New York Giants and Dallas Cowboys.

"You know what," he said, "I actually loved watching pro football for years. I remember the days when Jim Brown scored a touchdown and then handed the ball to the official. Like that. That's all. There was nothing special about that act, but seeing Jim Brown do it made it, for me. It was a piece of simple and appealing professionalism. I remember Jim Brown particularly because he ran with power and speed, but also with intelligence for all that force, 50 to 60 yards. The field behind him was littered with guys who tried to bring him down. They either got outrun or overrun. And then he gave the ball to the official and trotted off the field, as though this is what you're supposed to do when you're Jim Brown, score and bring on the kicker. There was no braggadocio. Just that.

"The celebration stunts you see today make me sick. I know they've toned them down. But it's not only the end zone acts. The rest of the grandstanding, like what you see after a simple tackle on the kickoff, makes me hit the surfer. Finally I said to myself, 'Why put yourself through this stuff?'"

"So," the customer said, "you now put on some tasteful Chopin when you're fed up with it."

"It's not that so much," he said. "I just got turned off by the game itself and pretty much lost the habit of watching it. That's not particularly logical, but I guess I just liked football straightaway without all of that posturing. There was enough in it that was exciting without the burlesque."

I didn't argue with John. How can you?

Most of the television watchers undoubtedly can live with the grandstand acts. But it's a fair guess that millions among them are annoyed if not offended or actually disgusted by them. The younger crowds, probably not so much.

Count me in the ranks of the offended. If you need specifics, put that vote somewhere between annoyed and offended. Save the disgust for Terrell Owens's rarer moments of narcissism, on the sidelines more than the end zones. I'm aware that open disclosure like this from old crocks attracts spasms of sadness from younger sophisticates, who will remind us that football is, after all, entertainment, and needs to be spiced up this way with some legitimate spontaneity.

Most of the acts that Owens pioneered have nothing to do with spontaneity. They were intended to attract cameras, whether he's badgering or humiliating his quarterback or coaches on the sideline, or turning the end zone into a circus tent, which was Owens's version of the hey-look-at-me theater that the network cameras still love.

This is not to say that in their time some of the end zone burlesques weren't amusing. There was a time when the Cincinnati Bengals were actually a good football team and when a rookie running back named Ickey Woods dazzled the audiences with what became know as the Ickey Shuffle, in which half of the Bengals' roster eventually joined. It got thick after a couple of years and the National Football League began formulating policies.

When they were at the height, lively arguments broke out over the true architects of the "ain't I great" celebrations.

They actually didn't start in the end zone. There is scarcely a fantasy footballer alive today who will remember the name of Mark Gastineau of the New York Jets. Yet as a pass-rushing defensive end, he was for several years the best in football. In 1984 he set what was then the league record for sacks with 22. He was 6-5, swift, powerful and nimble, weighed 270 pounds and in some games was absolutely unstoppable.

He was also roundly detested by some of his teammates, notably the defensive leader Joe Klecko. As a personality type, Gastineau was an uncompromising flake. After the fans began anticipating his pass rush, and the stadium's roar grew louder with each sack, Gastineau joined the euphoria. He didn't roar. He danced. He danced and flexed with the exuberance of an ancient warrior celebrating a kill.

The cameras couldn't get enough of it. The crowds, if they were Jets crowds, lapped it up. Some of his teammates, traditionalists like Klecko and Marty Lyons, were turned off. There were reconciliations afterward but injuries and a chaotic personal life together with problems with the law and drug tests shortened Gastineau's career. During the 1983 season, he and the Jets' quarterback got into a brawl. Gastineau was charged with assault, costing him 90 days of community service. He even tried professional boxing and actually might have been a successful heavyweight. He was that gifted.

But the curtain was up on circus acts that brought some of the daffier parts of pro wrestling into the arenas of the National Football League. The league began to frown, of course, but frown carefully, because a lot of that goofy narcissism was, and still is, popular with a sizable cross-section of the fans, particularly the home crowds.

The grandstanding era ironically might have had its origins in Green Bay, which is widely celebrated as one of the cradles of pro football but rarely linked with the stunts we see today. The hard-liner coach, Vince Lombardi, could hardly have been enthralled by the sight of Paul Hornung throwing the football into the highest reaches of Lambeau Stadium after scoring an ungodly number of touchdowns and field goals in the early days of the Lombardi regime. Years later the Packers—and the league—did condone the now institutionalized Lambeau Leap into the crowd by jubilant Packers who scored a touchdown. One of the Packer fans frostily explained the difference between the end zone burlesques and the Lambeau Leap: "There are stunts and then there's community-building," he said. "That's what we're doing with the Lambeau Leap."

The Packers' Greg Jennings basks in love after performing the Lambeau Leap. (Photo courtesy the Green Bay Packers.)

The league quickly black-flagged the ball throwing acts, but as television and pro football entered into their lucrative partnership, it was going to get grotesque.

For a while it was funny. Billy (White Shoes) Johnson earned his money in pro football primarily as a kick returner, but when he got into the end zone Billy wowed the audiences with what came to be known as the Funky Chicken, an act in which he waved the ball over his head while swaying as though entranced by the rhythms of soft rock.

Crowds lapped it up. Competitors materialized. For a few years White Shoes Johnson held the license, although the 49ers' Merton Hanks offered a passable refinement after scoring a touchdown. Bending his knees, Hanks did a duck walk through the end zone, flapping his elbows and swiveling his neck. For judges in this developing competition of football clowns, White Shoes Johnson's "Funky Chicken" suddenly seemed inadequate, so it became "The Rubberneck."

As the buzz among the fans got louder, some of the cleated thespians began looking for props.

One of the most cherished awards in football is the Heisman Trophy, given annually to the nation's outstanding collegiate player. The trophy itself is a statuette of a football player, ball tucked under arm, knee lifted high, and arm thrust out in the classic form of the old-fashioned stiff arm. It is such a visible icon on the American sports scene that while still playing college football, some of the hotshots in contention for the upcoming Heisman award candidly advertise themselves by simulating the familiar raised-knee and stiff arm recognizable to the football millions.

The standard-bearer for that particular act was Desmond Howard, who went into the pose after returning a kick 93 yards for a touchdown in his last game for the University of Michigan Wolverines. It either made him psychic or a great promoter because a month later he actually won the Heisman. Eventually the Heisman stiff-arm got into the repertoire of the merry pantomimers of the National Football League including, of course, Desmond Howard, who was voted the Most Valuable Player in Green Bay's Super Bowl victory in the 1990s.

The show biz acts multiplied and among the more recent was one by Wes Welker, the working man's pass receiver of the New England Patriots. In one of the Patriots' runaways last year, Wes playfully made a snow angel in the mounting drifts of the end zone after catching a touchdown pass. He was docked 15 yards by an officiating Scrooge and $10,000 by the league. Welker is one of pro football's by-the-book dependables, always there, almost always open, the soul of orthodoxy. But it was, after all, the Christmas season. He was contrite. He may, in fact, have been the only end zone performer in the history of the genre to seriously apologize afterward. "It was just a spur of the moment thing," he said. Something going to his head, probably about elves, sleigh bells, two feet of snow and a four touchdown lead. "It won't," he said, "happen again."

The deeper origins of the touchdown celebration cult have become a legitimate controversy among researchers. It's a common assumption that the stunts originated on the football fields of the United States, but Wikipedia will be the first to tell you that this is one more Yankee affront to our Canadian brothers. In the midst of a game between the Calgary Stampeders and the Saskatchewan Roughriders, a small corps of Calgary receivers celebrated in that glacier-sized end zone by converting the football into a simulated bottle of champagne, pretending to open the bottle, and taking a swig and then wandering off unsteadily but happily. In Winnipeg, the players are said to have formed a circle and then—after one of them threw the ball into the middle of it—falling backwards in unison as if blown away by a hand grenade.

The good news is that we haven't seen that one yet, but it's one you want to be aware of with some anxiety. If any wise guy wants to try that in the states, including the most recent end zone Houdini in Cincinnati, be alert. He might get carried away and try it with live ammunition.

The excesses of the American end zone routines were compounded on ESPN's Monday Night Football. There, Terrell Owens was featured in television commercials along with one of the stars from ABC's *Desperate Housewives*, who showed up in the locker room with a towel, which she promptly dropped before leaping into Owens's arms as though instantly magnetized. It was a sleazy act, and for a lot of viewers it crossed the line into porn.

By this stage in his career, Owens' credits in the field of noxious behavior were part of the daily sports page fare. Whether it was the 49ers, the Eagles or the Cowboys, it usually involved bad-mouthing his own quarterback for not throwing enough passes in Owens' direction. He took pains to do it in front of the cameras.

But it was the originality of his act after scoring that brought Owens his breakthrough notoriety. Playing for the 49ers against Dallas in 2000, he caught a touchdown pass, then pranced half the length of the field to stomp on the Cowboys' semi-sacred blue star at midfield. In Texas, this is like attacking the oil industry. The boos almost blew off the roof. To prove that this was not just a passing aberration, Owens did it a second time. All of which was the warm-up for his performance a couple of years later when he again caught a touchdown pass, yanked a pen out of his sock, autographed the football and ran to the stands to present it to one of his agents.

The NFL hung on gamely, cracking down on the stunts when they got too gross. But it was driven into a quandary by the league's ranking showboat, Chad Johnson of the Cincinnati Bengals. Johnson is that dread combinations of talents—he can catch and he's insufferable. He attracted massive audiences early when he and the Bengals were winning games. The midweek TV shows ginned it up. What was the screwball going to do next? Nobody was more versatile in convulsing the faithful. Johnson once pretended to propose to a cheerleader, getting down on one knee to implore. The NFL fined him for excessive celebration. He did an exotic dance. He did the Heimlich maneuver on the football. They kept fining him. He responded by hanging up a sign reading: "Dear NFL, Please Don't Fine Me Again."

They fined him again.

Two years ago he decided it was bland and unrewarding to go through life with the name of Chad Johnson. He changed it to Ocho Cinco. But when he wore the nameplate Ocho Cinco before the game, they fined him again because his name change had not been formalized and his last name, technically, was still Johnson.

The contagion extended to the more serious-minded of the NFL eccentrics. Late in a game against the Packers in Green Bay, Randy Moss, then with the Vikings, lowered his football trousers and mooned the booing crowd at Lambeau. It wasn't what you would call a Full Moon or a more memorable Autumn Moon. Maybe a Blue Moon. A Half Moon? How about How Low the Moon. Moss never came up with a convincing defense of this unfriendly act. It could have been a sudden stomach ache that required the loosening of all restraints. Whatever the pleading, the NFL wasn't buying.

Slowly, incrementally, the National Football League has brought most of these loony tunes under control, mildly upsetting some in the looser generations of football watchers who consider the zany stunts a harmless part of the show. To forestall the charge that the game is losing relevancy, the NFL does allow some reasonable grandstanding. No group performances are allowed. The penalty is 15 yards for unsportsmanlike conduct, which could kill you on the next kickoff. Harmless spiking or throwdowns of the ball are OK, as long as they can't be construed as taunting the embarrassed cornerback who was just beaten on the route. More permissible are the performances of pass rushers who crunch the quarterback and then energetically run 15 yards upfield while pounding on their chests to make sure everyone in the stadium and the TV audience at home can see who got the sack. Or they will paddle an invisible boat and combine multiple forms of these sideshows, which is what Jared Allen, the Viking sacker, has brought to the previously sedate and relatively unready state of Minnesota.

Most of these acts are heartily endorsed by friends of pro wrestling, which actually introduced the trappings of show biz to the American sporting public. Defenders of pro wrestling, which has now lifted comic barbarism to the edge of assassination, today maintain there is more posturing and show biz in pro football than there is in pro wrestling. They may be right. The one institutionalized gesture of triumph remembered best by pro wrestling fans comes when the victor or villain, throws his opponent through ropes and into the fourth row of seats. He then rushes to the center of the ring, thrusts out his chest, holds that pose for a full count of 10 seconds and then grandly struts around the ring to prepare the crowd for new triumphs. In pro football, most of the clowns who have just made a tackle for a 1-yard gain have that one down pat. They are always at their best and most lovable when they do it with their team trailing by three touchdowns.

No one in the NFL's upper suites knows quite what to do about the Lambeau Leap except to leave it alone. It's now in the public domain, although as much a part of Green Bay as Lombardi Avenue and bratwurst.

It can't shock you to learn that there are mildly conflicting claims over who created the tradition, which is: Packer who scores rushes to nearby stadium wall and flings himself into the arms of his adoring public. There isn't much question that LeRoy Butler, one of the Packer defensive backs, was the first leaper. In December of 1993, the defensive lineman and future Hall of Famer Reggie White picked up a Raider fumble and lateraled to Butler, who ran the ball into the end zone. In a book he later authored, Butler explained what prompted him to leap into the stands:

"Scoring a touchdown is exciting, but the anticipation of all those fans ready to thank you for what you have done gives you chills like nothing else," he wrote in The LeRoy Butler Story: From Wheelchair to the Lambeau Leap.

But it was an impulse. The fans were yelling. It was a clinching touchdown and Butler was aroused. This was togetherness—cheering fans and the winning athlete. So Butler started running toward the first row of fans behind the foundation wall of the stadium.

"Because I had pointed (that he was coming their way), the fans knew what they had to do," Butler said. "I jumped and got up into the green padding…and when I'm halfway up, a guy starts pulling me up the rest of the way. Everyone right behind him grabs on. Everyone is screaming and yelling. Some are complimenting me with 'Awesome' or 'Good job.' It only lasted 2 or 3 seconds, and I'm back down. It was an incredible feeling as I ran back to the bench."

So that is real. The star unites with his audience.

Do you like that? There is joy and spontaneity in it. Can it be overdone? It is, all the time. It's less than appropriate if done when Packers now trail only 35-7 But settle in. In Green Bay it's now and forever. The cameras by now have been hypnotized. They even delay the extra point. And if the Packers can do it, everyone else can. And some do.

Yet LeRoy's claim to spontaneous originality has been challenged by Terrell Buckley, another defensive back who played with the Packers. Buckley claims that he invented the Lambeau Leap when he and Butler were teammates at Florida State; LeRoy got the idea from him. He may right. So what? LeRoy's place in football history is secure. More so, you guess, than the Funky Chicken.

But watch out for those grenades.

8

Are We Ready for More Pro Football?

Pizza peddlers and telecom solicitors eventually have to confront the moral hazards of overkill. How much is too much?

Add professional football. It's a super-successful industry that has been inching its way around that same riddle for several years. Where do you stop?

Does America need—or can it handle—more pro football?

This is not a hypothetical question. Pro football IS going to expand its regular season schedule, probably to 18 games.

Why? Because it feels compelled to do something about the embarrassment of the four weeks of exhibition games before the season.

The most generous reaction to NFL exhibition games is to call them a fraud. If you want to come closer to the truth you can call them what they are—an extortion and swindle, a legalized act of robbery inflicted on people who buy season tickets to the regular season games.

After which you can poll the coaches and the players, many of whom will call the games not only worthless but hazardous.

Back in the days when players worked odd jobs in the off-season to pay the rent, the exhibition season served a purpose. Six weeks of training camp toned them up physically and the sequence of exhibition games gradually sharpened and polished their execution.

When big money overtook pro football all of that changed.

Weight rooms, lifting hardware and strength coaches came in. The business of pro football covered the calendar. It went from midwinter playoffs and the Super Bowl to the late winter combines to examining the hottest prospects for the draft, then preparations for the draft, the draft itself, mandatory or so called optional practices in the spring. The players' physical regimen changed radically. The summer workouts no longer were intended to peel off fat and stretch the muscles. In the summer the teams honed the offenses and defenses for the season. If you were a free agent rookie and out of shape for summer, you weren't getting past your medical. If you were a veteran you were smart by definition and you came ready. If you were a first round draft choice, you probably held out on the advice of your agent.

Most of the time, the record shows, it hurt your future in the NFL if you did.

Meanwhile, the NFL teams continues to stage its four exhibition games. The gamblers, of course, laugh at them because they aren't really a contest and therefore no bet. The coaches go through the required exercise of fielding a team, but mostly they hate the exhibitions because sooner or later one of their big guys is going to get hurt. It might mean a busted season for the coach and possibly his job. So they field the money players briefly and then get them out of harm's way as quickly as possible.

The players' reaction to the exhibitions is mixed. The veterans, meaning the bulk of the team, can think of better and safer things to do. Borderline players welcome them as a chance to make the roster. It's an obvious assumption but basically misguided.

The one clear benefit of the exhibition games in pro football is to marginally enrich the ownership.

Most teams in the National Football League sell their season tickets as a package that includes all of the home games—the eight regular season games and one or two exhibitions, which are also factored into the price although they're essentially masquerades. If you want assured seats for the regular seasons, you have to buy the whole package.

Angry and litigious ticket holders have taken the issue to court, claiming coercion, extortion or plain broad daylight theft. The court listens to their pleadings, sometimes sympathetically, and then throws the case out.

The bedrock reason is that nobody is forcing the season ticket buyer to buy the ticket. It's a package. You can buy it or not buy it.

If you want to buy single tickets to the regular season game, you can—if you get in line soon enough for whatever is available. And it very often isn't.

So the owners and the league set the terms.

The reason they've been reluctant to drop the sham of exhibition games is that they bring in extra revenue. Yet even the masterminds of the NFL agree that exhibition games have become an embarrassment. Game On: the first team plays for two series. Two and out. Second liners take over after that, and in the second half there's more excitement—from the standpoint of genuine suspense—at the bratwurst counter.

"I've been quite clear publicly and with our membership," said the commissioner, Roger Goodell, "that I think the quality of the preseason (the NFL still calls them preseason games and shuns 'exhibition') is not up to NFL standards, and that we should address that. So we're actively evaluating and considering whether we should modify that ratio and make it 17 and 3 as one example, where there's an additional regular season rather than the preseason game. We swap it out (with) the same number of games...I wouldn't rule out 18 and 2."

Eighteen and 2, of course, makes more sense than 17 and 3, which could drive the NFL schedulers—for all of their high tech calculus—over the bridge.

The coaches are virtually unanimous about dumping all of the exhibitions that they can.

"If you're talking about using the exhibition games to evaluate players," Bud Grant said "you lose me. The true test is in the summer practices. You find out who the players are in training camp, not the exhibition games."

So what about the old promotional pitches, "see NFL players battling for jobs?"

"If they're going to make the team, they're going to make it on what they do in the practices. Their most important battling is there. They don't all start from scratch, of course. A lot of those guys are regulars and you know about them. Sometimes you're a little shocked.

You draft a guy high on the basis of reports and information that you've compiled, and you just don't see that quality in the daily practice. What you see in an exhibition game can actually be misleading. You might have a defensive lineman who looked pretty good in the second half of exhibition games. The thing you don't know going into that game is who he's going to be playing against.

"If we had a defensive lineman trying to make the team, and he was matched against Ron Yary in some of the workouts and scrimmages, we had a pretty good idea what he was capable of doing in the National Football League. If he could look respectable and promising going against Yary, he was a guy to take seriously.

"The No. 1 priority of a football coach is being right in how he evaluates players. If you were going to base those decisions mainly on how a player looks in the exhibition games, you're on pretty thin ground. Yes, there are some benefits in those games, which are part of the business of sharpening up for the regular season, but you don't use them to pick your squad. Some teams will use their starters for two or three series and assume the other guys are going to do the same thing.

"We didn't go in for that. Before the game I told the players, 'We're going to play people in the order we want and for how long we want. What the other people do is their business.'"

Not all of the coaches, of course, looked at the exhibitions with the same detachment.

Grant's team played the Cleveland Browns in the annual exhibition game at Canton, Ohio, the site of the Pro Football Hall of Fame. Cleveland wanted to make a showing of which all Ohioans could be proud. The Browns played their regulars into the fourth quarter.

The Vikings started mixing their players in the first quarter.

The Vikings won the game.

The Browns re-configured their exhibition strategy the next year.

George Allen, who founded the future-is-now school of instant success, never saw a football game that he wouldn't scheme to win. In fact, Allen may have been the first NFL coach who campaigned to include the pre-season results in his won-loss dossier in the press book.

But surely there have to be some benefits coming out of these things.

"Not necessarily a lot," Grant said, "But sure, let's say you have a young quarterback trying to make the team and he's got some promise, and you've got a roster spot that's open. He knows about the intensity of the game from practice, but playing in front of a big crowd can get him conditioned to the pressure."

The players don't necessarily kiss off the exhibition games. They're paid, but nothing close to the money they're guaranteed under the regular season contract. There's a more fundamental reason. In their business it's never a good idea to be nonchalant in football's live action. One of the truisms in violent sport is that unless you play it full bore, whenever you play it, you're courting injury. Some players, the genuine football lifers, actually look forward to the action. Fran Tarkenton was one of those. Even later in his career he had no objection to going two quarters or more in an exhibition game. For Jim Marshall, football was football. There never was any bad time to play it.

The big hazard of exhibitions, of course, is injury to high asset players who can make the difference between winning and losing in the regular season. It's not the only hazard in taking exhibition games seriously.

In their earliest years, the Vikings struggled to make themselves relevant as a new franchise. Beating the Chicago Bears in their first official game in the league, 37-13, wasn't exactly a timid beginning. But they were still flopping around early in the exhibition games of 1963. Their third exhibition was in St. Louis, against the then-St. Louis Cardinals. Van Brocklin was the Viking coach. "We're starting right here," Van Brocklin told his recruits before the game. "I want you to hit and keep hitting and I want you to tell these guys you can play in this league."

So they came out hitting. They came out scoring. Tarkenton threw. Tommy Mason and Boom Boom Brown ran. Marshall and Rip Hawkins had the defense slashing. They did it in the first, second, third and fourth quarter, and they won the exhibition game 35-0.

The Cardinals were a team quarterbacked by Charley Johnson, one of the league's better ones. The great Larry Wilson was the safety. Pat Fisher played on the corner and Sonny Randle and Jackie Smith were receivers. The team eventually won nine games during the regular season, but in that August exhibition game the Cardinal regulars played only 10 or 15 minutes.

In September the teams met in Minnesota in the third game of the regular season. Wally Lemm was the coach. It's doubtful that Wally had forgotten the August exhibition game when the Vikings frolicked for five touchdowns.

This time the Cardinals scored early and they scored late. With a five-touchdown lead, and not a whole lot of time left, the Cardinals executed an on-side kick-off, recovered the ball and scored another touchdown. They won 52-14.

There was very little conversation between Lemm and the Dutchman when the game ended, as though any were needed. The message was as subtle as a kick in the teeth. The only commentary necessary was on the scoreboard.

But the exhibition idea, which made sense in an era when pro football was still virtually barnstorming, makes very little sense to most coaches today.

"When they switch to 18 games, as they almost certainly have to," Grant said, "they'll have to figure out how that's going to work out in the budgets. The owners like the present arrangement because they've got a good thing going. But they'll have to rework the player contracts because they'll be playing more games, and the players association will have something to say about that. That means only two exhibition games, with one at home. So you know where the season ticket prices will be going, and the fans may have something to say, too.

But the revenue from the networks will go up for sure. That's another negotiation. But it will come.

And sages will warn that pro football is walking a dangerous road as it approaches or exceeds the saturation point. That's a hypothetical point, one assumes, beyond which the paying sponsors may grow leery and the American public begins to ask a question: Hey, how far do you go with this?

And about this time the public survey experts who track the American tastes in entertainment will probably look at the TV audiences as well as the stadium attendance at the end of the 2009 season and say. "What's everybody worried about?"

Some shows don't need a whole lot of fixing—as long as there is a psychiatrist around nearby if the millionaire owners and the millionaire players decide in their negotiations next year that they can't possibly agree on how to keep the best show in town from shutting down.

In that event, a good place to start would be getting rid of the exhibition games, which almost nobody loves and adding a couple that count—which will undoubtedly sell out like all the rest.

9

How Tailgating Became
Godfather to Fantasy Football

Accountants insist that only certified billionaires can own a professional football team in this country.

Maybe. But there are millions of people in America who insist they know how to run a football team. When you think about it, it's thrilling. An untapped higher wisdom lies ready and able to solve all available problems in operating a football team and lifting it into the Super Bowl. This wisdom is sitting there in thousands of sports bars on Sunday afternoon, waiting to be summoned and joining the invisible oracles who call in or flood the internet. You can call this an unsung triumph of the American dream that at this very moment there are armies of unlicensed football masterminds waiting to offer their bumbling football team a clear road to glory.

Rarely has one national sport, pro football, become so intimately interwoven with its public. World soccer may be the only one comparable. It didn't happen overnight And the personal and public identification between the fan and the game may actually have developed its momentum in the rough-hewn society of the mass tailgate parties, which we'll explore in a minute.

One direct outgrowth of all that mushrooming involvement is Fantasy Football, which hinges on the performances of offensive stars in actual games and gives millions of people permission to act as surrogate coaches. It has now, in fact, become a national institution, in turn sprouting parallel industries. Advising Fantasy coaches on who to play at running back this week is a thriving business on radio. The real-life games themselves trigger volunteered wisdom or loathing from hordes of listeners and viewers across the country each Sunday. Radio call-in shows offer a handy megaphone for fans betrayed by the bumpkins of the home team. Sports columnists are flooded with emails from yet another sector of public involvement, the internet, where the public's wisdom breaks through the dikes.

But generations ago, this primal urge to community among the football watchers took root in the stadium parking lots. Maybe there is something in the dynamic of football that links the game, in a noisy but rather appealing way—with the impulse to gather together in a communal herd, with radios blaring, barbecue fires blazing and beer flowing bountifully. You could, in fact, go all the way back into the frontier days of the West, when the trappers and hunters and ped-dlers got together in weeks-long grog and trading parties called ren-dezvous. Eventually they lost out to modern competitors called towns and stores and civilization. When the rural gatherings got calmer they were called hoedowns or the tamer quilting bees. In time the automo-bile and outlying stadiums arrived, and with them airport-size parking lots. So did the outdoor cookers and bratwurst accompanied by thou-sands of merry-makers, and the tailgate party was launched.

In Minnesota, when the Viking games were moved to a domed stadium in downtown Minneapolis, honest-to-God tailgating van-ished and much of that sense of festival disappeared. It also happened elsewhere around the league. Sprawling parking lots—the natural habitat of tailgating—have been largely lost to eight story ramps and Wal-Marts and Targets. Attempts have been made to keep the spirit alive near urban stadiums, but the old parking lot atmospherics can't be convincingly replaced by tailgating under a circus tent.

For a lot of these displaced persons the sports bars are a social-ly acceptable substitute for the vanished camaraderie of the stadium parking lot. Consider the sports bar: Here, fans with swivel necks and an insatiable craving for Nacho chips can watch six pro football games at the same time, plus the Boston Celtics and the Minnesota Wild, and the odd pro wrestling match from Atlanta for those grooved on the ultimate mayhem.

The sports bar is comfy and neighborly but it's not genuine tailgating, which needs an unfenced range. Tailgaters instinctively need to stroll and roam and feel loose and unbridled. Most of them are inquisitive and eager to butt in on the party in the next lot, where they are drawn more by the aromas than the off-key guitar played the bratmeister, who wears a Rack the Pack battle cry on the back of his purple jersey. This is what people do at these things, or in Minnesota what they used to do in the parking lot. Today outside the Dome they scrounge for cheap tickets.

The long-gone Metropolitan Stadium on the fringes of Minneapolis still stirs the golden-agers of Minnesota into spasms of mourning. Put me in their company, although I'm not totally sure why. The parking lot needed two hours for traffic to clear when the game was over. The custodians learned quickly to open the gates before daybreak for a noon game. Hundreds would be crowding the gates before sunrise, competing for the friendliest parking stall. The idea was to avoid the crush of departing vehicles after the game. Sobriety tests would have produced enough arrests to gridlock the exits. It didn't happened. The outmanned cops were too busy trying to break up potential open warfare among the crowds of drivers trapped in three exit gates that were supposed to serve 45,000 people.

Amazing sights were on view routinely in the Met Stadium parking lot on game day. A large camper-trailer full of Viking fans from northern Minnesota drove in at mid-morning for a Viking-Bears game. Both teams were contenders at the time. The game commanded wide attention around the country. Anticipating that, they had collected prime tickets from season ticker holders unable to attend (or happy to sell the tickets for a few hundred big ones). I was covering in those years and was alerted to the tasteful furnishings in the camper-trailer from northern Minnesota, including a large TV set installed for the pre-game run-up on national television. The partiers heartily welcomed the visitor. We talked about the buildup to the game and their eagerness to drive 800 miles round trip to see it. Their party was going full bore, the parking lot was jammed and the game was a half

The days when the hibachi cooker was King.

hour away. I wished them luck and walked to the stadium.

An hour and a half after the game my work was finished and I headed for my car. En route I spotted the camper-trailer where I'd left it. It had been a terrific game and, feeling sociable, I knocked on the door. Camaraderie and the familiar scents filled the trailer and I asked whether the fans enjoyed the game.

"Couldn't be better," the head man said.

And how were the seats, I asked,

"What seats?"

"Your seats for the game."

Silence. After which: "You know, when you left," the man said, "the party was just getting started. We thought about it and decided to watch the game on national TV."

"Here in the van?"

"Right. We had everything we needed right here. Grilled hamburger, fries, real comfort, great conversation."

"But you came 400 miles—"

"It'll be 800 miles round trip, actually."

"But you could have watched the game on TV back home."

"You could figure it that way, but we had the best of all worlds this way. I admit it wasn't the plan. But the more we thought about it the more we figured, 'why not stay in the van? We had a warm and comfortable place to watch the game, good conversation, plenty of eats—plus we could hear the roar of the crowd in the stadium, practically on our doorstep. I don't know how you can get any more realistic than that."

It may have been the actual birth of Reality TV.

At one Monday night game I got to the stadium after finishing a two-hour call-in with Howard Cosell on a radio show. My plan was to ease my way back into reality after Howard. I'm not sure I found it. This was in September, a time of the year when it was relatively common for couples attending the game to bring a folding snack table for a light supper before the kickoff. A section near the center entrance gates had been roped off for this kind of pre-game pastime. The impresarios at the Met were thoughtful folks. Like all longtime observers of the Met Stadium tailgate culture I'd experienced novelties to end all novelties in the Met parking lot but I wasn't quite prepared for this. A man wearing a black tux with boutonniere and gold shirt cuffs was holding his wine glass and toasting the woman seated opposite at the table. She wore a full-length gown of white with something close to a tiara in her hair and a look of quiet adoration.

A burning candelabra bestowed a dignified warmth to the scene, especially after the musicians from the nearby Viking longboat finished their pregame rendition of "Go, Vikings Go."

I stood nearby long enough so that it was impossible to mistake my interest and approval. The woman was generous. "Care to join us?" I pleaded lack of time but asked what was the occasion. "We're in love," he said. "Have been for years. We hope to marry soon and we do this every year in anticipation. We're also football fans. The Vikings usually win when we do this."

He raised his glass, she raised hers. "To us," he said. She nodded and smiled.

"Lovely," I said. "All you need is appropriate music."

He dug into his brief case and came out with a tape recorder. "We were just about to play it." He punched a button and set the volume discreetly. The wistful chords were familiar.

"Do you know it?" he asked.

"Second movement from Rachmaninoff's Second Piano Concerto."

"We play it every year."

I thanked them for their time and walked into the stadium. The ticket attendant was one of my favorites. "Neat, that couple out there. You think they'll ever get married?"

"Probably. The thing is they re-enact this every year and the Vikings usually win. They're in love and they don't want to change their luck, so they're still single."

The Vikings lost and I never saw them again. Which, if you are a romantic, was probably a good sign.

Yet this was not the most novel scene of blossoming love in the Met parking lot, which, incidentally, was fully capable of matching the soap operas. Its most thrilling happening may have been the actual wedding in the Kansas City lot performed by one of the community's esteemed judges, The Honorable Spike Lommen.

Friends had arranged a New England shore dinner of lobster, baked chicken, sweet corn, baked potatoes, pink Chablis and three kinds of oysters. It was relatively modest fare when measured against the tailgate standards of the 1970s at the Met. But both bride and groom confided they planned to spend the first stage of their honeymoon at halftime in a Winnebago camper rented especially for the occasion.

After the game some of the reporters ignored the football stars leaving the stadium and rushed to the Winnebago. Probably influenced by the football writers' practice of assigning credit in a winning performance, one of the attendants in the party talked about the performance of the judge. He sounded serious.

"I think Judge Lommen did a tremendous job out here today," he said. "It was easy to overlook in all the excitement. I liked the part when he came to that 'love, honor and cherish.' There were all kinds of distractions. The Viking band was playing 'Skol, Vikings, Skol' someplace inside the stadium and Paul Flatley was on the radio doing color on somebody's transistor. The judge outlasted them. He even played the wind right. It started up about the time they played the wedding march. So the judge had the rice-throwers move behind the Winnebago and make their ceremonial tosses from there, with the wind."

Clearly this was a bravura performance by the judge, to say nothing of the newlyweds' loyalty to the game by emerging from their brief honeymoon in the Winnebago in the first half and joining their pals in the bleachers.

These things actually happened during tailgates in the Met parking lot.

The money in pro football may be on the nation's television screens and the glamour may be on the field. But when you think about it, no matter its origins, the parking lot picnic before and after a football game clearly satisfies the irresistible craving of today's football fan to get immersed in the action. In Green Bay and in Bloomington, the site of the old Met Stadium, you had the Super Bowl and Mardi Gras of the tailgate scene. This was only partly explained by the parking capacity of the lots. One of the visiting writers a bemused Californian named Bob Oates of the *LA Times*, said he was convinced that in mapping the earth's land mass God plainly envisioned the Midwest prairie as one unbroken stadium parking lot.

Arguments that threatened to become actual brawls sometimes broke out in the Minnesota-Wisconsin border communities over the comparative class and grog capacities of the tailgate crowds in Green Bay and Bloomington. Actually, they were about even under polar conditions despite their annual commemoration of the Green Bay-Dallas playoff game of January, 1968, which finished with the mercury at 17 below zero and undetermined number of fans welded to the stadium by their backsides.

This is hallowed stuff for Wisconsin crowd, but Minnesota fans are not stampeded by that performance. Their argument: While the temperature got to 17° below in that game in Green Bay, the wind was not much more than a mild breeze, blowing at 13 miles an hour from the northwest.

"No tailgate crowd has ever equaled Minnesota's performance in 1970," a season ticket holder told a New York television reporter. "On two consecutive home games we tailgated in a windchill of minus 35° and a windchill of minus 28°. Anybody can do this once. It takes real guts and Minnesota character to repeat."

Possibly. It was in Metropolitan Stadium where the Vikings' first NFL divisional title game was viewed in entirety from a 50-foot-high snowbank beyond the stadium walls, but with a great angle of sight overlooking the end zone.

Nobody in town can tell you whether the Vikings are still going to be here beyond 2011, when their Metrodome lease runs out. They may get their new stadium in the heart of Minneapolis. It depends on fate, Ziggy Wilf, the legislature and probably some new economic rescue package.

If they do, it ought to be remembered that you can't tailgate in the lobby of the IDS Tower.

10

The Mixed Thrills of
Coaching in Today's NFL

Most schools in America conduct a job fair to introduce the country's next wave of entrepreneurs to the beckoning doors of lifelong success. Rewards are promised to imaginative minds. Recently, hedge funds have been avoided.

The usual rewards are good pay and longevity. A comfortable quality of life is often an add-on. Fame and a worry-free old age are occasionally offered as inducements.

The job of head coaching in the National Football League almost never makes an appearance in these display booths.

The obstacles to joy and adulation in this field include impatient owners, a 3-13 season, eccentric receivers and unforgiving season ticket holders. You can add free agency and the salary cap. These are so daunting that nowhere will you hear promises of lifelong fulfillment at the coaching lodge's recognition banquets.

Most of them get fired sooner or later and sometimes often.

It does pay well, considering. But while you're considering, note that the funereal procession of freshly unemployed head coaches begins when the National Football League season ends.

Nobody's feelings are spared. Appeals to logic and recent success are enthusiastically ignored. What have you done yesterday? The Super Bowl? That was three years year ago. You may have won the Super Bowl but you're dead meat if you missed the playoffs—again.

While the traffic in bummed-out coaching reputations is brisk and predictable, the line of wannabe successors remains congested.

Elbows tend to be sharp in that line. If pro football has become the royalty of bigtime sports in America, the annual changing of the guard among the coaches at season's end is now becoming less ceremonial and a lot more ruthless.

Within three weeks in January this year—the mere three weeks it took the Arizona Cardinals to reach the Super Bowl from their habitual role of an unloved mediocrity—these things happened:

The New York Jets fired Eric Mangini four months after presenting him with Brett Favre and the keys to Manhattan.

The Tampa Bay Buccaneers fired Jon Gruden, who won the Super Bowl for them not that long ago.

The Cleveland Browns fired Romeo Crennel, who was hailed as a defensive genius when they ransomed him from Bill Belichick.

The Denver Broncos fired Mike Shanahan, who had coached them to not one but *two* Super Bowl championships.

The Detroit Lions, reaffirming their claim as the most screwed-up franchise in professional sports, released Rod Marinelli as a simple act of mercy. This came after the unsalvageable football team presented to Marinelli by the Lions' management lost all 16 games on the schedule, a feat once considered beyond the reach of mortal men.

But some NFL brain trusts refused to get caught up in the unsightly stampede to the scaffold at the end of a season. They got an early start on the dirty work. The San Francisco 49ers got rid of Mike Nolan and the Oakland Raiders did the same with Lane Kiffin a few weeks after the season started.

Not be outshone, the St. Louis Rams dumped Scott Linehan before Halloween. To prove this was no fluke, the Rams did the same to Linehan's successor, Jim Haslett, but stuck with tradition by doing it on the familiar Black Monday, the day after the season ended.

All of the departed were quickly replaced because reorganization for the next year begins the day after Black Monday. There is an added incentive to hire next year's coach early. Nothing sells better in professional athletics than hope. This usually materializes in the form of a new head coach when a losing team approaches its fans and the ESPN panel shows before Draft Day. The words of George

Allen are prophetic. For coaches in the National Football League the future IS today.

So why would anyone of sound mind want to coach in the National Football League?

Begin with money. You can make millions of dollars as a head coach in the National Football League If you're just starting out they usually have to give you a few years' grace period to develop your program, which means guaranteed millions. (In the 1950s and early sixties a head coach in the NFL earned $35,000 a year.)

During the flurry of expulsions at the end of the season, assistant coaches pass one another in the airport terminals as they fly off to interview for one of the vacancies. During the process the surface courtesies are publicly observed. Coach Leslie Frazier, the defensive coordinator for the Minnesota Vikings, was invited back for a second interview by the St. Louis Rams. Local newspapers spoke respectfully of his chances. So did the Rams. Frazier sounded confident.

Steve Spagnuolo of the New York Giants got the job.

By all accounts Leslie Frazier was, and is, a highly desirable candidate for head coach, having been part of the Vikings' emergence as one of the strongest defenses in the league. Employing people like Pat and Kevin Williams in the middle probably helped. Mike Tomlin, Frazier's predecessor as the Viking defensive coordinator, became the Pittsburgh Steelers head coach a few years earlier and quickly took the Steelers to a sixth Super Bowl championship in 2009.

Frazier was interviewed for several head coaching jobs after the 2007 season and again this last season. The list includes Denver, Atlanta, Miami, Detroit and St. Louis. The problem with being publicly identified as a failed suitor is that sooner or later the decision-makers are going to ask themselves: "Why is this guy still available?"

Frazier, highly competent, remains an appealing candidate—for now—but all assistant coaches suffer from recurring anxieties that the head coach they work for might not be around next year, and an incoming head coach is likely to surround himself with a new set of favorites.

Which means that on a grander scale, employment in the National Football League is almost never secure. The true and blooded professionals in head coaching are usually spared that discomfort and, of course, have earned it. In the midst of the 2008 season, Mike Holmgren announced his forthcoming retirement, opening the door to the younger of the two coaching Jim Moras (the elder Mora had retired from coaching for the more comfortable role as one of hapless coaching foils in the Coors Lite ads on TV.) Within a few predictable months Holmgren was allowing that yes, under certain conditions, he would entertain another coaching job.

It almost never ends.

Tony Dungy, a Super Bowl winner and now a genuinely revered figure in National Football League coaching as well as in the broader range of human affairs, retired at the end of the 2008 seasons to be succeeded by one of his assistants, Jim Caldwell. Will Tony be back some day down the road?

Probably.

But when a newcomer arrives on the scene as head coach, a lot of the incumbent assistants start squirming and looking elsewhere because the incoming coach is scanning a field of applicants he may know a lot better. And, of course, he has his own preferences going in and pretty well settled by the time he's announced. So the competition in coaching at all levels in the National Football League is lively and more or less endless. On the other hand, there ARE jobs. Fifty years ago most National Football League teams maintained a staff of five or six assistants. There was a defensive line coach, an offensive line coach, a receivers coach, a backfield coach (who was also the quarterbacks coach) and possibly a special teams coach.

In 2008, the Minnesota Vikings, to take a convenient example, had more than twenty coaches on the staff. Beyond the incumbent head coach, Brad Childress, the supporting cast included:

Offensive coordinator, defensive coordinator/assistant coach, assistant special teams, special teams coordinator, coaching assistants in charge of running backs, head defensive line, assistant defensive line, tight ends, assistant defensive backs, head offensive line, assistant offensive line linebackers, quarterbacks, wide receivers defensive backs, head strength and conditioning coach, assistant strength and conditioning, assistant strength and conditioning, assistant wide receivers, quality control, offense, quality control defense, offensive/defensive assistant, assistant to head coach, coach's administrative assistant, assistant to Brad Childress. Two or three of these positions are essentially administrative. The others number approximately 22, directly involved in the team's preparation for next week's game.

All of these people undoubtedly deserve every dime they make. Why?

Because pro football is rich enough to pay.

And why are there so many?

Because almost everybody else in the National Football League is doing the same thing.

What if Team A reduced the number of assistants to 10 and had a good season?

The rest of the teams would hire 22 to get ahead.

What if Team A won the Super Bowl with 10 assistants?

The rest of the teams would hire 22 to ambush them with numbers the next season.

Clearly most people in the National Football League believe that winning the Super Bowl with only 10 designated assistants, which the New England Patriots do with some regularity, is an aberration.

The Patriots' website lists 10 assistants. It's possible that when Charlie Weiss was coaching Belichick's offense before going to Notre Dame, and Romeo Crennel was coaching the defense before going to Cleveland, they weighed so much that the rest of the league was counting three coaches for Charlie and two for Romeo. And it's likely that the Patriots have people behind the scenes assisting the assistants, people not formally counted as assistants. And it's probable that the reason Belichick can win with fewer assistants is that he is a secretive guy anyway and doesn't need them. Besides, a lot of his players have been there so long they know more than the assistants.

The revolving door of head coaches and the proliferation of assistants can result in odd scenarios. For example:

Three years ago Ken Whisenhunt and Russ Grimm were members of Bill Cowher's Pittsburgh Steelers coaching staff, which won the Super Bowl in 2005. Cowher retired two years ago for the quieter battleground of the TV analyst panels.

Whisenhunt applied for the vacant job. So did Grimm, a onetime star lineman with the Redskins. One of his teammates in Washington was Ken Whisenhunt.

Neither got the job. It went to the defensive coordinator from Minnesota, Mike Tomlin.

When nobody could win as a coach at Arizona, the Cardinal management decided to try the energetic job-seeker, Ken Whisenhunt. With him came Russ Grimm as an assistant. On the day the Cardinals earned a berth in the Super Bowl under Whisenhunt (and Grimm) the Steelers did the same thing in Pittsburgh. So the melodrama continued, and two weeks later in Tampa Bay, Tomlin ultimately emerged from the soap opera as the Super Bowl winner.

Although analysis abounds, no one has been able to pinpoint a personality or professional trait common to all successful professional head coaches.

Vince Lombardi won in Green Bay. A hard man. A driver. A good coach and a winning coach who deserves his honors, said Bud Grant, "but a tyrant."

Grant rarely characterizes other coaches. He had personal experience dealing with Lombardi, when Lombardi was at Green Bay building a team and Fuzzy Thurston was in Winnipeg with Grant's team. Lombardi wanted Thurston in the NFL. As Grant remembers, Lombardi didn't ask to make a deal for Thurston, he demanded it. Grant's response: Slow down and talk civilly. Grant ultimately set a figure as fair compensation to his club and Thurston went to Green Bay as a cornerstone of a great line.

One of Vince's veterans was asked the key to Lombardi's dominance of the game for a half dozen years. "Maybe it's how he handles people democratically," the player said. "He treats us all the same, like dogs." Nevertheless they played for him, and the ultimate cachet of their pro football careers, many of them acknowledged then and still do, was the respect they earned from Vince Lombardi.

The two coaches met twice during Grant's first season as the Viking coach in 1967. Grant's team was evolving, and the offense had a long way to go. Lombardi's teams had won the National Football League title the two previous seasons. Grant's team won only three games that year. But one of them was in Milwaukee where Grant and Lombardi faced each other, and Bill Brown went in from a yard out to give the Vikings' a three point victory. They lost to the Packers by the same margin in Minnesota in December, less than a month before the Packers defeated the Cowboys for a third straight NFL title in the game later immortalized as The Ice Bowl.

Vince Lombardi

At the time the Packers were on a roll, having won the first two Super Bowls against the recently organized American Football League. The two leagues later merged, after Joe Namath and the Jets had beaten the NFL's Baltimore Colts in what is still the most famous—certainly the most shocking—of all of the Super Bowls. (Grant's first Super Bowl team lost to Kansas City in January of 1970 in the final match between the two leagues before they combined to form the present NFL.)

Lombardi was gruff and impatient, yet the charismatic commanding general of his forces. He had, in fact, worked with Col. Red Blaik of the Army football team at West Point before moving into pro football with the New York Giants and then the Packers. He was a perfectionist in almost every corner of his life. The archives don't record it, but there was an unprogrammed but revealing snapshot of his character one day in the 1960s when he brought the Packers to a Saturday morning practice session at the old Met Stadium for a game with the Vikings the next day.

We'd talked several times by then, and had a reasonably cordial relationship. Typically I called him the Monday preceding the Viking-Packer games, and was conditioned to the usually terse if marginally responsive answers to the questions.

"Understand Paul Hornung is injured," I said on the field that Saturday. "I don't see him out here for practice. Is he going to be ready?"

"Paul Hornung," Lombardi said, "is always ready." It was an answer which incidentally could have been provided by Hornung's latest girl friend as well as his coach. But Lombardi was right and Hornung played well the next day. What I remembered from that Saturday was Lombardi's scene with a local television reporter. The reporter's channel was not part of the network televising the game. It did have sports shows and a regular sportscaster, who happened not to be working that morning. The station needed a clip with the visiting coach, so it assigned a young man who knew football, but not very well. He boned up in advance but his day was busy and his prep time might have been confined to a few minutes between a beauty pageant and an overturned semi on the highway earlier in the morning. He waited patiently for the practice to finish, then introduced himself as Lombardi was walking to the team's dressing room.

"Can I have two or three minutes with you, Coach?" he asked.

Lombardi said yes, he could give him some time.

The camera's red light went on and the young reporter began with the predictable queries about tomorrow's game. Lombardi answered them. The reporter then asked if he expected the Vikings to work any special defenses against one of the Packer receivers who had scored three touchdowns in the last two games. He identified the receiver.

Lombardi stopped the interview, and the reporter could thank God that the interview wasn't going live. Lombardi actually took the microphone out of the reporter's hand.

"Tell me something," Lombardi scowled. "How can you not be prepared? That player was injured and we announced three days ago that he's not going to play. How am I supposed to answer that question if you're going to air this interview? I'd have to say on the air that this guy is not going to play and everybody knows it."

He chewed on the shaken young reporter for a full minute. There were only the three of us, but you had to feel sorry for the kid. And then Lombardi did something I liked and didn't expect.

He lectured the young man in a tone something close to a father's.

"You can do better than this," he said. "I realize you have other things to cover, but pro football is pretty important in this town and you have to do your best to get it right. I'm not telling you how to do your business. I'm reminding you that you're in a competitive business just like we are in pro football. The first step is always to prepare yourself. You have to be ready, even for a three-minute interview. Sometimes especially for a three minute interview. Now I'm going to talk to this fellow from the Minneapolis newspaper for a few minutes and then let's do the interview over."

We talked and, curious, I stayed to watch the TV redo.

The kid handled it without flaw. When it was over, Lombardi shook his hand, said "Thanks and good luck," and walked away.

The kid floated to his car.

Lombardi could have sent the young man packing and told him to come back next year when he'd learned how to set up for an interview. He didn't. He taught. And he probably saved the kid's job.

Years later, remembering that story and in the midst of a profile on Bud Grant for the newspaper, I thought about doing a little mischief and asking him how he would have reacted in the same situation.

I never asked him. First, Grant as a coach didn't deal in many hypotheticals. So I constructed one privately. The kid fluffs the question. Grant doesn't call his attention to it. It was just some misinformation that coaches deal with all the time. Grant keeps going with the interview, says something suitably ambiguous, tells the kid he expects a tough game because this is a rivalry, and the interview is over.

In the context of finding the common attributes of successful football coaches, some of them now called great, the more you think about the Lombardi and Grant match-up the more tantalizing it becomes.

Lombardi was viewed as the super-coach of his time. He had a compelling personality. He would glower and harangue, challenge and goad. The Packers would fumble for the second time in three series. The TV cameras come in tight on the fuming mastermind walking the sideline in his camelhair coat. If you read his lips he is saying—so the rest of the bench can hear it—"What the hell is going on here?" Van Brocklin in his snarling genius for defamation called Lombardi "that goddamned spaghetti eater." But one day in Green Bay, when Van Brocklin's underdog team beat Lombardi's champions in a nationally televised game, Lombardi walked down to the Viking locker room and met Van Brocklin as he emerged. Lombardi shook his hand and said, "Your team played a great game. It's a tribute to you, coach."

Van Brocklin almost welled up in gratitude.

You could not have written pro football through the latter part of the 20th century without encountering most of the best among the coaches. My informal list of the best in the last 50 years would include, in no particular order, Paul Brown, Bill Walsh, Grant, Lombardi, Bill Belichick, Don Shula, Bill Parcells, Chuck Noll, Tom Landry, Joe Gibbs, Mike Holmgren, Andy Reid, Tony Dungy—and if you want a man who was a decent coach and a good guy, add the running game-loving Chuck Knox, the well-known Ground Chuck of the Los Angeles Rams, among others.

Most of these people had strong and driven personalities and some of them were flinty, overbearing or neurotic. Stereotyping them may not be the wisest or most generous way to make an assessment. You could probably use the same labels for any given class of banking executives, university presidents or Army generals. Grant could be kind and even emotional about giving an extra year's contract to a veteran player who was going downhill but who had delivered the best he could give for nine or ten years. It's called loyalty, and hard-headed football coaches sometimes nurture that quality even though it's not always visible to the fans.

If you were asked to come up with a word to associate with Bill Belichick of the Patriots, the long-running model franchise in the NFL you might start with abrasive, and then move on to surly. Or how about sociopath? But then read Belichick's response when Scott Pioli left the Patriots to become the general manager of the Kansas City Chiefs. Belichick and Pioli had worked together for 17 years, first in Cleveland and then New England. It was Pioli who had pulled most of the strings in assembling the kind of teams Belichick could turn into winners. He was for years the personnel chief with the Patriots. The two had been friends.

When Pioli left, Belichick said:

"To sum up in words everything Scott Pioli has meant to this organization and to me personally would be difficult, if not impossible. From the day I met him, he has demonstrated a passion for football and respect for the game that is second to none. Working side by side with one of my best friends for almost two decades is special enough in itself. But to help each other achieve success beyond our dreams is a blessing and something I will always remember and appreciate."

It's all right to take another look at Bill Belichick.

Lombardi, too, was a hard-bark guy, often quick to judgment, but also a man who did not blush to be called a celebrity. Paul Hornung told of visiting Lombardi after the coach had come out of retirement and coached the Washington Redskins for a couple of years. Lombardi invited Hornung to dinner at a popular DC restaurant. As they were walking to their table, Lombardi in the lead, the more than a hundred diners stood and an applauded.

"Paul," Lombardi said, "how do you like it? This town is full of some of the most powerful people in the world, and these people stand up and applaud a football coach?"

"The Old Man pretended to be surprised," Hornung said. "He wasn't. He loved every minute of it and would have been disappointed if it didn't happen."

Grant clearly would have been surprised if it happened to him, and he seldom if ever put himself in a situation where people sat and stared.

But he won. And there were reasons why he won that went beyond the enlistment of high quality players and an effective coaching staff.

Those reasons are worth examining.

"The first thing I learned when I started coaching," he said, "was that there was no way I could change who I was, no matter what I did in coaching, and the habits I learned early stayed with me. I was a product of my times, going all the way back to the 1930s when I was a kid and we had very little money in the family. I didn't get a nickel from the folks because they needed all we had just to get by. It those years, it was "here are a pair of pants and a couple of shirts." That was it. I remember seeing my mother counting carrots and rutabagas when she was cooking meals. I got one cookie after every meal. My bed was a couch. In those years, when you were 16 you had to start bringing money into the house. You also had to figure out a few things about life."

Like competing. Grant was an athletic prodigy—football, basketball, baseball. He even played hockey until he was 14. What he learned early was how to win.

And how do you do that as a coach?

"I learned early how not to do it. I remember Bernie Bierman, the University of Minnesota coach, showing us films of one of his championship teams and how they ran the off-tackle play or the buck lateral, and the first thing I learned about that was how worthless those old films were to the here and now. The offenses and defenses were different ten years later.

"I played hard and for keeps. It was the kind of mentality I carried into coaching. And I found out pretty quickly that the only way I was going to be worth something as a coach was to keep myself under control. I know there are coaches with hot tempers who have been great coaches. I couldn't do that. I've got Jerry (Burns) up there in the booth yelling down some play, and we're sending players in and out and I can't manage the show if I'm running around screaming at the officials."

So let somebody else do that.

How credible to the team was Grant, almost stationary on the sideline, calmly working his headset, translating Jerry Burns, getting the play in?

Jim Marshall, the durable defensive end who played almost forever, marveled at his coach.

"Old Bud," he said, "was a winner. The players knew that. I always said that if I ever found myself trapped in the jungle with lions out there someplace, and I had my choice of one guy to get me out of there, the guy was Bud Grant."

There were stories about Grant's quiet and selective discipline in the locker room. "If the player was important enough," the stories went, "Bud found a way to exert selective discipline."

Grant has heard all of the stories and doesn't give them a whole lot of credit.

"One way to avoid the traps of how to enforce rules," he said, "is not to set up many rules. And we didn't have all that many. Yes, say a fine of $50 (the rates of the '70s and '80s) for being late to a meeting. You have to be sensible about it. Yes, there are reasonable excuses. After a while you run out of reasonable excuses. So the player says he's late because he had a flat tire. I explain that I've have heard the flat tire story before, and I have to tell him I'm a coach, I'm not in charge of flat tires. There's a meeting, and you have to find a way to be there."

"You had to be fair, to try to treat the players equally, but you had to make exceptions, too."

Was it easier for the coach to make exceptions when the player might be the difference between winning and losing next Sunday?

Bud Grant rarely falls for a sucker play. He'd had a few disagreements with Alan Page, his greatest lineman, a man of independence and values of his own. Later in his career there were practices Page did not attend.

"He was studying for a law degree," Grant said. "He knew what he had to do to be ready for a game. That included working on his own. If a player like that asks to be excused from practice to attend class, I'm going to excuse him."

Adjourned.

The Vikings' Williams Wall, Pat (94) and Kevin (93) Williams, maul Detroit's Kevin Smith.

Doing it all! Antoine Winfield sacks Jake Delhomme, forces a fumble and runs it into the end zone.

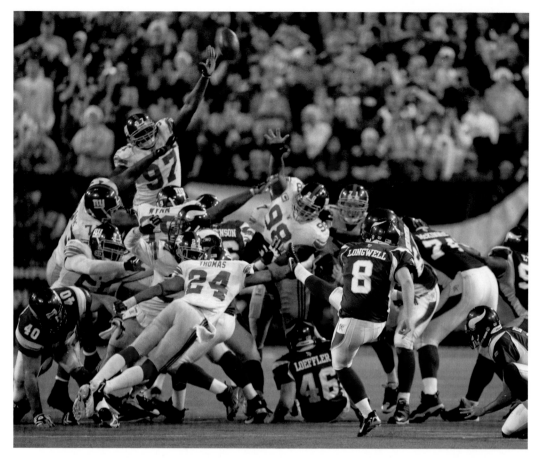

Ryan Longwell's 50-yard field goal with time expired eludes the fingertips of the Giants' leaping Mathias Kiwanuka (97) to propel the Vikings to the NFL's 2008 Northern Division title with a 20-19 victory.

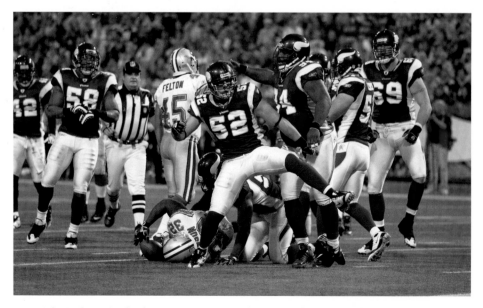

The Vikings' Chad Greenway (52) celebrates after the defense overruns the Lions' Rudi Johnson.

In today's pro football, EVERYBODY gets in on the action.

Adrian Peterson meets his public.

1) Adrian Peterson turns the corner after breaking a Packer tackle.

2) Brad Childress checks his omni-present play list.

3) On his way to the Hall of Fame, Randall McDaniel (in 1989) clears the way for Allen Rice (36).

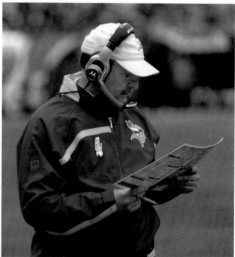

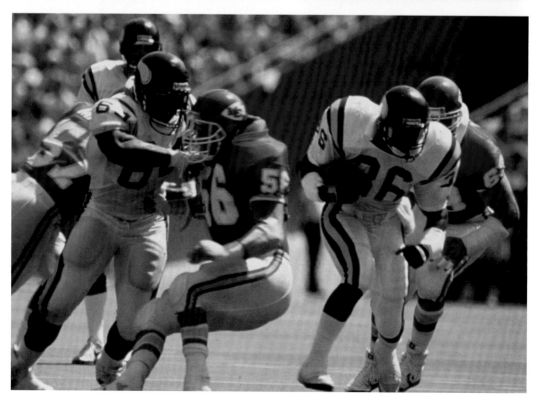

For the memory book: 1) Bud Grant muses. 2) Fran Tarkenton buys time.
3) Alan Page and Jim Marshall (70) meet at the quarterback. 4) Ahmad Rashad's
end zone spectacular.

A formidable front line.

The Vikings' Jared Allen engulfs Arizona's Kurt Warner.

For the memory book: 1) Bud Grant muses. 2) Fran Tarkenton buys time.
3) Alan Page and Jim Marshall (70) meet at the quarterback. 4) Ahmad Rashad's
end zone spectacular.

A formidable front line.

The Vikings' Jared Allen engulfs Arizona's Kurt Warner.

In his best years with the Vikings, nobody equaled Randy Moss's catches in thin air.

Adrian Peterson with a few Chicago defensemen in pursuit

Walter Payton in action

You can call that eclectic coaching.

Which translates into "Whatever works." Grant mastered the craft.

"I think that most successful coaches have to build up some kind of trust, so that the players see they are being treated as human beings with values of their own. And you don't have to be a hugger to do that. I think I had that kind of trust from most of my players. I had a reputation of being cold-blooded in player decisions I made, but you HAVE to make player decisions. That's the core of the job. You can be decent about it. It's one reason why I insisted on talking to each player who was being released when we had to cut down. A lot of coaches don't like that part of it and don't do it. But I have to tell that player the reason or reasons. It's something I owe him for his effort. He may have made pro football the ambition of a lifetime. I need to tell him that I respect that ambition, but we can't keep every player who tries out. Sometimes I can encourage him to keep trying, maybe with another club. Other times I'm not doing him a favor if I encourage him to keep going, so I won't.

"And once in a while I was rewarded for that. I had a talk with a kid who was one of those All-American human beings, but wasn't going to make it quarterbacking in pro football. I told him we were impressed by him in almost every way—his work ethic, his mentality, his attitude, all of those things. I said I was sure there were a dozen other directions where he might want to go, and I would bet on him to make it.

"It broke his heart to walk out of there.

"But years later I got a letter from his wife. He'd gone into business and made every one of his goals, had a great family, traveled the world and employed a lot of people. His wife said he had never forgotten the conversation we had when he left the team. She said that was an hour that shaped his life. She said he was convinced that what he learned that day he carried with him for the rest of his life and the confidence I'd expressed in his character and his commitment to a goal guided every major decision he made after that training camp.

"When you coach for as many years as I did, you get satisfaction in seeing your players succeed not only on the football field but in what comes after that, and what it represents is a gift later in life, that somewhere along the line you've done some important things right.

"If you've been in the business long enough, sooner or later you also find yourself being some kind of therapist. I've had women come in to talk to me after finding lipstick on their husband's shirt and wanted to know if I could talk to him. I don't think I had any training for that, but you do have to try to understand the people you meet in this business, and sometimes their problems."

He took wholesale ribbing when he came down from Canada. His players were startled when, on one of the first days of practice, Grant introduced a drillmaster who was going to teach them how to stand at attention for the national anthem, as a team.

It was all over the locker room in five minutes. "We don't know much how to get into end zone," one of the team's comedians said, "but we do know how to salute."

It wasn't exactly saluting. "It was something I'd noticed early in football, that guys just sort of stand around where they are when the band plays the national anthem. I didn't care for that. I thought we should show some respect for the flag and to the crowd, also."

After a few weeks, they had it down: helmet held at their hips, feet lined up on the sideline, heads-up, the full team forming a straight line.

The crowds appreciated it. In time the players valued it. And in a few years, the Vikings were getting phone calls from other NFL teams, asking how they organized their players for the national anthem.

"OK, it was a small thing," Grant said. "But it seemed like the right thing, and eventually the players not only did it but wanted to and it made them feel, one of them said, a little more together."

So the truly memorable coaches march to their own lights and cadence: Lombardi was stirred by the gods of perfection and often got there. He was a winner of Super Bowls. Grant, molding a team, picking the right players, calm and in control, keeping them together; a winner of championships, four times in the Super Bowl, but not a Super Bowl winner. And after all of those years, retiring in contentment to his family, his duck blinds and his hunting dogs.

What are the qualitative differences between their coaching careers?

None that matter much. Both of them are in the Hall of Fame.

Do the Super Bowl losses still grind on Grant?

"Well, no. To stay healthy and productive in this business you have to learn to live with losing. We lost to great teams in those games. In a couple of them, one or two plays early made a difference. If you want to know if I still look at the films of those games now and then, the answer is 'You can't be serious.' I still run into Marv Levy at times (the Buffalo coach whose teams also lost in their four Super Bowl appearances.) Fine guy. He's doing well and obviously adjusted long ago to those Super Bowls. We're a pretty good contrast. I love responsible hunting and fishing. It's a big part of my life. Marv is an animal rights activist, picks up stray cats and that sort of thing. The last time I saw him I told him I killed four deer out west. He almost chokes when he hears that."

Ever wonder what would have happened if they met in a fifth Super Bowl?

11

A Blizzard Schooled a Hall of Famer

In the lore of the American north country, the Armistice Day blizzard of 1940 is called the Storm of the Century. It struck in early November and it was lethal and paralyzing.

The warning systems were primitive, nothing like today's satellite imagery. The storm swept rapidly through the Upper Midwest, marooning thousands. Many died. The storm was racing full fury, still a couple of hours away from northern Wisconsin, when two teenage kids rowed their duck boat across the lake near the town of Webster for an afternoon of hunting. The weather deteriorated quickly. In a few hours the howling winds and driving snow turned their hunting interlude into a fight for life.

They struggled back to their cabin through freezing wind. With the wind coming hard and driving sheets of snow, the 14-year-olds had no chance to row back to their cabin and instead walked back through an icing swamp. Part way to the cabin one of them was unable to continue, clothes frozen so solidly he couldn't bend his pants legs. The other plodded on toward the cabin where they and an older friend planned to spend the night. Eventually they were able help the other kid to the safety of the cabin, but by now fingers were so stiff they couldn't hold matches to fire up the cabin stove. After massaging their hands long enough to get a fire going, they pried their way out of their clothes and wrapped themselves in blankets. With night approaching, the storm abated but the countryside by now was an unearthly landscape of monster snow drifts. After regaining their strength, they left the cabin and returned to the car they had driven from their home in Superior, Wisconsin, and managed to get it going, bulling it through the heavy snow of the country road with muscle as well as gasoline.

Within an hour they found themselves stymied by several stalled cars in the road. The stranded occupants were struggling to stay warm, knowing they weren't going to move any further in that wasteland of packed snow.

It was night and the road was impassible. One of the 14-year-old kids got out of the car, opened the trunk to put on a pair of waders and headed out into the night to find help. To conserve fuel, the others shuttled from car to car, sharing body heat and keeping the engine going in one or two while the others were shut down to conserve gas while they struggled to get through the night.

To the shivering people in the cars, the 14-year-old who went alone into the night had the look of somebody who knew what he was doing despite his youth. He was a big kid, plodding through the snow, looking for signs of civilization. He walked for miles. He saw no buildings and no lights. Nothing showed.

He kept walking. Finally he came to a snow-covered building, which turned out to be a country store. The woman proprietor said, "Come in and get warm." She had no electricity but there was a stove, and others were coming. There the kid spent a snowbound night, in the store, unaware of the fate of the others but knowing they could get by with their shared fuel several hours into the morning. At daybreak in the wake of the storm he headed back to the stalled cars. By then the stranded party had been spotted by a deer hunter who lived near the scene. Together all of the now-combined refugee party, the teen-kids, their friend and the other motorists, made tracks for the deer hunter's sanctuary through the drifts. They stayed for two nights. Nothing was moving in the vast white-out. And then they heard the sounds of motors: Snow plows coming and from Superior, a fire engine with its crew.

All survived.

Is there something in this story that could foretell a scene more than 50 years later when a football coach renowned for his self-control in the midst of tumult around him would stand to be inducted into pro football's Hall of Fame?

You'll probably not be surprised to learn that the kid in story was Bud Grant, and that he behaved in that crisis about the way he handled himself in that win-or-else Roman Coliseum of American coaching, the National Football League. Or that one of the rescuers in the fire engine crew was his father, Harry, a fireman.

The relevant question is: what does it take in the crisis.

Consider the shaky shelf life of coaching success in the NFL today. Consider, also, that the gladiators in the Coliseum may have had it easy.

The only thing they had to worry about was hungry lions.

In the middle of the 2008 NFL playoff season, the country's sports pages were crowded with the professional obituaries of head coaches whose failures had offended the club's ownership, the fan base, some of the media scholars and the blogosphere—not the mention 30,000 season ticket holders.

That is an impressive roster of head-hunters. The sins of the departed coaches filled the usual rap sheet. The coach missed the play-offs or lost control of the game or the sidelines. Or he fell in love with the draw play on third and 4. Or he wasn't temperamentally suited to deal with prima donna players making more money than he was.

All of which makes the Harry Peter (Bud) Grants of the world rarities that need to be explored and, above all, consulted.

Grant retired after a comfortable career of nearly three decades of more or less uninterrupted success as a head coach. He won in the National Football League and in Canada, in the cold or heat waves, under domes and on frozen grass. He won as a player and a coach, from the 1940s into the 1980s. As a player he won in basketball in the Big Ten and with the Minneapolis Lakers in the National Basketball Association. He won as a tight end (or any other position they wanted him to play) in Philadelphia in the NFL and later with the Winnipeg Blue Bombers in the Canadian league. The teams he coached won the Grey Cup in Canada four times, reached the Super Bowl four times in the NFL, and won 11 division titles and four conference or NFL championships in advance of the Super Bowl.

Linebacker and defensive play-caller Jeff Sieman confers with the Viking staff.

Nobody fired him. He won everywhere he went, but managed while doing it to disclaim any symptoms of genius. He did have the sense to give full range to the skills and drive of the players he led and counseled, to maximize those skills and to keep the higher demands of the team in the forefront.

What kind of players? Begin with Alan Page, Francis Tarkenton,

Ron Yary, Carl Eller and Paul Krause, all of them—like Grant—now in pro football's Hall of Fame. Add Jim Marshall, Ed White, Mick Tinglehoff, Chuck Foreman, Jeff Siemon, Bill Brown, Ahmad Rashad, Gene Washington, Karl Kassulke, Paul Dickson, Matt Blair, Scott Studwell and a few dozen more.

He avoided inspirational speeches, which would have been out of character. He gave the appearance of unchanging stolidity and devotion to habit. He didn't spend much time diagramming plays. His coaching assistants produced the so-called game plans, the strategies, formations and play sequences based on the usual exhaustive film studies. Grant functioned as a kind of hands-on executive officer, and no one ever doubted who was in charge, least of all the players. His football values and his evaluations of his players and the temper and commitment of his team were present in every game. He didn't bother denying wisecracks about his devotion to habit. He did suggest, here and there, that one of those habits was winning.

He left the game with the respect of a generation of former players who admit never quite understanding how he won, or what it was about Grant that made them feel they were not going to lose a game because of over-coaching or some bonehead decision on the sideline.

He never apologized for not winning a Super Bowl. He did offer one possible explanation that had clearly eluded a generation of fans—that the other teams just might have been better.

But when you examine the public afterlife of some of the great coaches—many of them jockeying today in front TV cameras but marking time for the next ripe coaching proposition—another question surfaces: What was the toll on a guy like Bud Grant from decades of cutthroat competition at the highest level of professional sports?

The answer is: What toll?

Here is a man with a lifelong commitment to the virtues of calm and order, which for Grant has been a code of conduct since adolescence. Being calm and orderly and controlled on the sideline might have some connection with the disciplines he acquired in the woods and lakes where he fishes and hunts. And today wild nature is a replenishment for him, that and his public advocacy for the preservation of clean waters. But well beyond that is his dedication to family as the core of his life and the ultimate gift in it. It touches almost every day of his life after football. From the beginning of their marriage, he and his wife, Pat, had never been more than a half-hour drive from any of their six children and now the swarms of grandchildren. That closeness and comfort of family became the surmounting gift and solace for him when she died this year. They'd been married for 59 years. She was a volunteer and a support in a dozen causes and social needs, and when she died thousands joined the family in the celebration of her life.

So there has been family and the outdoors for the retired coach, the hugs of grandkids, the football he still follows, and the frequent renewals with some of his old friends from the duck blinds and athletic arenas, the late Billy Bye, Jerry Gruggen, Bob McNamara and others. Football today also means watching the performance of the high school team coached by one of his sons, Mike Grant, for years one of the most successful in the country. He admits they don't wear out the dinner talk discussing strategy or technical football, partly the generational thing but also temperament. The last thing Bud Grant is going to do at 82 is to tell somebody else how to coach, particularly Mike, who practically grew up in a locker room and was a ball boy for Viking teams when he was a kid. The old coach marvels at both the quality of high school football today and at some of the coaching it receives. Pro football, of course, still engages him. He watches it in the stadium and on television, and knows both its excesses as well as its excellence and mounting appeal.

"It's still the game," he says. "In a lot of ways a better game and a different game. The times are different. I don't spend a lot of time judging it."

When he coached he rarely raised his voice and never used profanity, and is annoyed by some of the language he hears today. He's no preacher. It's simply who he is. Nor did he feud with the news guys or romance them. He gave most of them the time they needed and never ostracized them, regardless of the quality of their reportage or commentary. But if the question was impertinent or self-serving he would drill the interrogator with a silent stare that pretty well throttled him for the next couple of weeks.

So what was it that thrust this man above almost all of his contemporaries in three decades of coaching? You have to first set aside one of those urban myths about coaching in pro football. Being calm and controlled doesn't mean a man goes through life as an emotional cipher. Grant was not that, nor is he. But among the emotions he avoided were rage, jealousy and egomania, all of them somewhat counter productive if you want to win football games.

His game face and demeanor invited the whimsy in his players, writers and spectators. We needled him about his sideline rigidity after somebody was inspired to describe the atmospherics there as Grant's Tomb. But he was always civil, and as the years passed an admiration grew among the press corps for Grant's greatest strengths—his ability to choose and assemble quality players and keep them grooved on a goal. Add the ability to keep himself and these highly individualist athletes under control. His teams generally were free from the curse of the star system, although the team had many stars. Add to his absolute dedication to his personal values.

"If I had any advantage once I got into coaching," he said, "it probably came from my playing days from high school to college and into the pros. I had the kind of physique and maybe the disposition to play almost anywhere. I played tight end, wide receiver, linebacker, cornerback, lineman, fullback, just about the works. I played both offense and defense. I called plays. All of that helped me later to evaluate players or to put them into a niche that gave them and the team the best chance to succeed. I could see the mistakes they were making and suggest something better. All of those things are very much a part of coaching and were even more important in the earlier days when you didn't have the big staff of assistant coaches you have today.

"So you have to be good at recognizing genuine talent and whether an individual is going to be a winning ballplayer. You have to go beyond physical ability or physical potential. How is this guy going to fit into a team or in the locker room? Is he so good that you can accept some of his negatives as a personality, or can you do something about changing those negative?

"But there's no instant formula in predicting a successful future for a coach. One thing he needs (in short supply in the 21st century) is patience to make himself better. Technical knowledge is just not enough. I remember in my earlier years sitting down around a big table with a bunch of relatively young coaching assistants who could regale you with their football knowledge and all the new language and schemes coming into the game. I couldn't get in a word edgewise. And I'd have to ask myself, 'Where did all of that come from and where is it going?' I had to step back and ask myself what are the absolute musts in coaching and in being the leader. It finally comes down to having confidence in the decisions you make, knowing you can't possibly make the right ones all the time, but being comfortable that you know how to win, that you have given the players the tools to win. They also need to know that you don't have to go crazy when you lose.

"In today's pro football you can't be successful, the champion, year in and year out. The NFL aims at trying to equalize competition. It does that with the draft, scheduling polices and the salary cap, all of which penalize winners.

"One my good friends is Bob Knight, the basketball coach. We've hunted together and share some of the same outlooks on coaching."

An aside here. Those shared traits probably don't include temper control. The thought of Bud Grant sailing a chair across the bow of an astigmatic line judge is almost too scary to contemplate. But there is no question about their mutual regard.

"We were talking about judging players and I told Bob that I never minded when a day of hard rain meant we couldn't practice at our training camp in Mankato, because on those days we'd sometimes go into the gym and play basketball. That surprised him and he asked why. I said I can tell a lot about football players when they're playing basketball. We'd divide up the players into teams. You can find out something there about the competitive attitudes of athletes, I mean hard core competitiveness. You can see things about quickness when they run the floor and you can learn something about their personality traits, and especially whether there was something ingrained there about accepting the idea of team.

"A football coach's relationship with his staff is critical. I think one mistake a lot of coaches make is to hire their friends. When I became a head coach I had a lot of friends who were in the business and were good coaches. I didn't hire one. It wasn't any personality thing. When I looked at it I thought this: 'This is a friend of mine. I know what he knows and vice versa. I want somebody who knows what I don't know."

Is that pretty calculating? It is. It was also one reason why, following his predictably rocky first season as the Vikings' coach, that Grant brought in Jerry Burns to overhaul the Viking offense. The team was in the playoffs the next season. The following year it was in the Super Bowl.

Like all successful coaches, Grant had a serviceable ego, which was a long way from conceit and clearly warranted by years of success as an athlete and head coach. "Were in the entertainment business," he said. "We're also in competition. To be successful in this business you have to know who you are and who you aren't. I was a coach. After you put in your time learning what works and what doesn't work for you and the team, you should reach a certain confidence level—some people call it a comfort zone—that tells you what you can do and what you should not waste time trying to do. We spend the better part of the week preparing for Sunday. All of the important work you do with the team should be over on Friday. It was for me. I didn't want to spend the rest of the weekend before the game agonizing over whether we were ready or if there was something more to learn."

So on a Saturday afternoon, with Big Sunday on the horizon, Bud Grant would often go hunting.

Why should all of this have been so amazing?

"I learned pretty early that as a practical matter, you made the important decisions during the week on how you were going to play the game, what you were going use, the situational options that you had, the tendencies of the other team, its strengths and weakness. All of that went into what people came to call the game plan. The staff signed off on it. One way or another you had to feel good about it, and the one thing I knew for sure was that it was the best thing we could do. Second guessing myself was not something I wanted to drag myself into. It was also pretty much part of my nature. It involved the conscious decisions you made, evolving decisions made with the staff, players buying into it. After that, I thought it was useless to spend time worrying about it, reworking it or agonizing over what the other team was going to do. You can go crazy doing it that way; or at least it was the way I looked at it. There's only so much you can do as a coach."

So sometime around 5 p.m. on Friday, the players were gone, Grant locked his office and went home to feed his hunting dogs.

But there were (and are) coaches who keep a cot and a supply of anti-sleep potions in their offices. These are props for the addictive anguish of endless preparation—last minute film-watching or working the play sheets. On a Thursday before a big playoff game between the Vikings and Washington Redskins in Minnesota, I called the Redskins public relations office to arrange for a five-minute interview with George Allen, the ceaselessly scheming Redskin coach. George was one of my favorites. He was a football lifer but accessible, always returning calls. He was cunning, usually a winner, and unstoppable in his quest for an edge. George originated "the future is now" cult of eliminating the so-called rebuilding year. He surrendered draft choices ruthlessly in return for the fading skills of another team's aging star. He was also insatiable in spending the house's money for state-of-the art training facilities. Edward Bennett Williams, the late Redskin owner, knew all about George's modus operandi. During Allen's first season in Washington, Williams was the speaker at a business luncheon, and somebody asked him for a brief progress report on the state of the ball club, competitively and financially.

"I'm not sure I can tell you," Williams said. "When George signed on, we gave him an unlimited budget—which he exceeded in his first three months."

I wrote for the Minneapolis afternoon paper at the time and calculated that with George's habits he probably would make the call at 8 p.m. Friday at the earliest, which would give me plenty of time to go in early in the morning and do the story for the Saturday afternoon edition. He didn't call by 8 p.m., or 9 p.m. or 10 p.m. or midnight. I knew the story was shot because the night was gone; Allen hadn't called, and he was certainly not going to be making calls early in the next morning in time for our crowding deadline.

At 3 o'clock in the morning my home phone rang. "This is George," he said. His voice had the sound of a tone-deaf frog. "I'm sorry to be calling at this hour. We had some late stuff to go through and I'm just finishing up here, but I want you to know that your call is right there at the top of my list." I asked a few questions. Allen actually asked more, just skirting inside the edges of propriety but insisting that he wasn't fishing for information on the condition of Chuck Foreman's knee.

" George," I said, "I couldn't tell you."

"You know," George groaned, "we're pretty banged up."

"I heard."

We talked for ten minutes and George was responsive enough. When he was finished I said, "Get some sleep."

"Right," he said. "I've just got a couple more things and then it's lights out. Been a long day."

Twenty hours worth.

Grant won most of his battles with George, but not many came easily and he enjoyed the encounters. One has to share a final sentimental snapshot of George the strategist in action. The Vikings and the Los Angeles Rams were going to lock up in a playoff game during the Christmas season in the lovable old rattletrap of Metropolitan Stadium. George was coaching in Los Angeles then. The Rams hated to play the Vikings in the cold. When they arrived two days before the game, the Twin Cities were smothered by a snowstorm.

Both teams had to practice in facilities away from the stadium. The Rams were quartered in a hotel in suburban Bloomington the night before the game. Worried about the emotional condition of his players, removed from their families at Christmas time, George scheduled a team Christmas party.

The morning of the party I got a call from the Rams' public relations man. "George would like to have a few kids to join us in the party," he said. "George likes the idea of giving the players the feeling of a typical Christmas Eve, a tree lit up, carols during dinner, kids sitting with the players, that kind of atmosphere. Do you know where we could locate some kids who would like to join a pro football team at a Christmas party?"

I thought about it, not especially surprised that George would want to orchestrate a Christmas party for his warriors. But I agreed with the PR man that it would be great for the kids.

I called the supervisor of a home for boys, and he liked the idea. He put it to the kids, and eight or nine of them happily volunteered to join the players.

The Rams PR guy called the next morning. "It was terrific," he said. "Great idea. The kids loved it and the players loved having them."

How about George?

"Well George greeted the kids warmly. But he spent the whole night sitting alone at his table, doing Xs and Os on his scratch pad while everyone else was singing "Jingle Bells" and all the rest."

Grant thought it was a great idea himself, but the Vikings did beat the Rams the next day.

Among his traits as a coach, Grant brought a passable interest in the psychology of the game, and he took George to be one of the guys who couldn't walk away from the game. So he wasn't surprised when George, after retiring from a Hall of Fame career in the NFL, returned to college coaching at Long Beach State. His players drenched him with the customary sideline frigid shower when he won his last game. Afterward, reporters asked for his response to the soaking. "You'll notice it was icewater," he said. "We couldn't afford Gatorade."

George didn't do comedy as an acquired trait. What he was as a coach, besides knowing his craft, was an angle-player and a confessed perfectionist who was neurotic about being ready and having his team ready.

Bud Grant followed a different light. He was aware that his self-control cast an image. He knew that his face-on-Mount Rushmore demeanor on the sideline made him a target for gags and lampoon. It was a pose the fans loved.

"Well, that was me," he said. "I didn't need a show of emotion to tell people that what was happening out there was important to me. So many people in our business are concerned about image. I had this image but I didn't invite it. If you create it, it's not you. I think one advantage I had was that the players knew who I was and what I thought was important, both in the game and in life. I was going to be the same coach next year as I was this year.

"I coached against a lot of personality types. Most of them were good football men but some of them were conscious about other parts of their personalities and needed to project themselves. I coached against one guy who knew he was going to be interviewed by TV before the game and he came with as much make-up as Mae West. He had a silk suit and tie and fragrant foof all over himself. I told myself this guy is getting ready for television as much as for the football game. I remember talking to him before the game and he kept looking around for the cameras.

"He didn't win a lot of games. He didn't win any against us."

When Bud Grant finally retired from coaching—but kept his home in Minnesota and his fishing and hunting cottage in northern Wisconsin—there was no mass mourning in the cornfields but a sociable acceptance around the state. The coach had put in his time, had been straight with his teams and the fans, and probably could fill out on walleyes a lot faster than Vince Lombardi. To understand the coach-and-public relationship, you have to know Minnesotans as folks who can get a little giddy over the return of dull gray normalcy.

Other places demand electricity from their heroes. Bud Grant meant comfort. He was shag rugs and woolies on a cold night. How many people do you know who will vote against comfort? With Grant coaching, the ball team was orderly, never unsightly and practically always in the playoffs. He meant comfort because under Bud Grant the football team was a football team and not a disconnected gaggle of showmen.

Somebody asked him a question, this old football warrior in a Marine haircut and swamp stains on his shoes. Did winning a title rejuvenate him?

Grant dissected that question silently for awhile and then said that he never felt UNjuvenated. Naturally, everyone went wild from Lake of the Woods to Winona.

Grant's old quarterback, Joe Kapp, had been right. There ain't no red-nosed reindeer flying from chimney to chimney. But there is still Fort Knox. And Bud always admired bullion more than rooftops. The risk of a losing season couldn't have occurred to him. Grant was that rarity in the steam cooker of pro athletics, a man serene with his private lights and therefore unterrified by the thought of losing a football game. Because he was one of those who lives within himself and has come to terms with his limits and his ambitions, he rarely tortured himself over professional or personal decisions.

For a long time his peculiar virtues as a human being weren't as recognizable to the audiences as they were to his players. He looked impenetrable, icy, and unfeeling. The players have always seen him, though, as a person of balance, shrewd enough to know that winning comes faster to players and coaches who keep their emotions under control. They also know he was as motivated to win as any coach they ever saw. Athletes often live in turmoil, imposed either by the crowds or by themselves. Those who played for Grant came to respect the even rhythms of his coaching style and his personal codes. Whatever happened in life or on the field, his family truly came first. It's why after a football game played and coached at the highest level, he could leave the stadium and drive home to play pool with his kids and eat ice cream. The players trusted him in the decisions he made and the values he seemed to express.

It's why a Grant or a Tom Landry or a Don Shula would win on Mars if they put a franchise there. Their commitment was steady. So were their nerves and their discipline. Players see that. The security and self-control that coaches like Grant reflect impresses ballplayers, partly because most of them are insecure, no matter how great.

A few years after he retired, the electors in Canton ratified the player's judgment. They voted into the Hall of Fame this sensible man who knew how to win, how to survive a lethal blizzard and how to avoid the allure of self-glorification.

And more than 20 years after he retired, his friends gave him a party on his 80th birthday. And why should it have been a surprise that more than 2,000 people came to join the celebration?

12

Sometimes, Just Listen to the Players

Yes, there *was* an Otis Sistrunk who smoked cigars and played football like a bald-headed bouncer, and there *was* a Doctor Death.

And maybe it's time to exonerate the felonious old Oakland Raiders and tell them they are missed.

Pro football today is a five-star production with audiences approaching 100 million. But the Raiders of Al Davis's most menacing years deserve an airing if for no other reason than their novelty as blowhards: their big talk matched not only their arrogant dispositions but their performance. They won. And they DID play like pirates. They talked the same way, baiting their opponents before the game, and taunting them from start to finish. They were incorrigible and hilarious; which reminds us that when you remove the professional football player from the grind and clamor of the game itself, the personality you uncover may be a lot more vivid than the helmeted warrior you see crashing and banging on Sunday afternoons. And nobody had more personalities per square yard than the Raiders.

Pro athletes often adopt a fatalistic cover about winning and losing. Most of them understand their vulnerability. In their more relaxed attitudes away from the battle, they sometimes expose a side to their nature that the stadium-goer or television-watcher never sees or hears. It can come in wisecracks or bitterness. But some of the most revealing sides to the ballplayer's mindset surface when he has time to reflect or to express the streak of mordant humor that's a lot more prevalent in the players' psyches than most fans realize.

139

That may be one reason to remember Otis Sistrunk and the Oakland Raiders.

John Madden was the coach-overseer of the Raiders during the years when they were viewed as a gang of incorrigibles on probation from house arrest. Otis Sistrunk was one of the first of the aggressively bald-headed football players. He was described in most of the clippings as The Man From Mars. The title was bestowed on him, possibly in envy, by Alex Karras, the notorious defensive lineman of the Detroit Lions back in the '60s. Sistrunk was huge, hostile and generally unmanageable on the football field. He also smoked cigars.

In the run-up to the Raiders-Vikings Super Bowl game of January, 1977, Sistrunk called the journalists to order at his interview table a few days before the game. He was asked to forecast the outcome. Sistrunk slowly disgorged a volley of cigar smoke and spoke.

"Those Vikings are fine, God-fearin' fellas," he said. "It would be nice if they could win a Super Bowl game, real nice. That team has so much, but it has misfortune. I know the first thing you fellas from the press want to know is what kind of misfortune. I'll tell you. The Vikings misfortune is they got to play the Oakland Raiders. I wish there was some comfort I could give the Vikings, but there ain't. People ask me, how can you beat Francis Tarkenton and the Vikings with a three-man line, and I say, "Man, we ain't got a three-man rush. We ain't got a four-man rush. What we got is an eleven-man rush. It may not show in the films, but it shows in our hearts."

I offer these lines as a lament. Pro football today gives us a thousand thrills, courtroom sideshows and playoffs lasting through time. But it can't reproduce the Oakland Raiders of the years when Al Davis ran his halfway house for rehabilitated sociopaths—and it's a loss to be mourned. In those days spontaneity was still available. The characters of the game seemed a little more, well, original. With the exception of the Super Bowl, they were not as visible through TV interviews, websites, blogs and other high tech vehicles for self-promotion. And it may be that because few of the players were millionaires in those days, they were less self-protective.

Whatever the reason, the Raiders were an irresistible bunch. No football organization today could possibly assemble a team to match Al Davis' Raiders in its potent mix of athletic prowess and pathological destructiveness. For talent it had Kenny Stabler, Fred Biletnikoff, Dave Casper, Art Shell, Gene Upshaw, Ted Hendriks and Phil Villapiano. For mayhem it had people like Sistrunk, Jack Tatum, John Matuszak, Charles Philyaw, Skip Thomas, and George Atkinson. An observer said the Raiders drew their talent equally from the colleges and the late night horror shows. They called Thomas "Doctor Death." Atkinson was so belligerent that one rival claimed he played like the Godfather's hit man executing a contract. Chuck Noll, the Pittsburgh coach, was so incensed in his complaints that Atkinson filed a multi-million dollar lawsuit against the coach and a newspaper. All survived.

The Raiders objected to all of this as raw defamation. One of their spokesman before the Super Bowl that year was Upshaw, the cerebral and talkative offensive lineman who later become the head of the NFL Players Association.

"I don't apologize to say it," he said before the game, "but we've got a helluva bunch of linemen. In Oakland they pay their offensive line. Other guys run and pass, but tell me where Paul Revere would have been without a horse. The trouble was Paul Revere got more ink than the horse, but with our outfit the horse might have been the one they wrote about. I'm going against Alan Page. Great football player. He claims I grab and hold. The only guy who grabs better is Alan Page. Watch him Sunday. He'll do that. I see Alan says he doesn't cheat in line play. He claims he's a moralistic player. We ain't going to church Sunday. We're going to the line of scrimmage in the Super Bowl. There's a difference. I'll tell you they can talk all they want about the Stablers and the Tarkentons, but it's the Upshaw and Pages who win the Super Bowl

"The quarterback, he may be the Willie Shoemaker if you want to compare football with a horse race. Upshaw? He's Secretariat."

The newly licensed thoroughbred paused to consider.

"I just wish I had Secretariat's stud fees."

The assembled scribes in unison offered their sympathies to Upshaw.

As it turned out, the Raiders' Secretariat won has handily as his predecessor. It was 32-14 at the finish.

So the times were a little different. Spontaneity was available. The characters of the game seemed a little less self-oriented. And you did them a favor by giving them a platform where it made sense to produce some reasonable theater. How could you resist talking to a player like Nate Allen, who was a reckless cornerback with the Vikings in their big years. He was no Hall of Famer, but he made himself valuable, remembering Bud Grant's maxim in evaluating players. Nate called himself The Junkman." "Bump and run, I can do that man. I'm available. Blocking field goals, turn me loose." During one critical afternoon in a playoff game at Metropolitan Stadium, the Rams stormed inside the Vikings 10. But there, Page, Eller, Marshall and Gary Larsen said, "no more." The Rams hit three times into the line and found themselves two feet from the goal line. By then the Viking defensive linemen were the "Purple People Eaters." The Rams didn't trust themselves to advance two feet against Page, Eller, et al. But they didn't want to come out empty, so they went to the field goal. Nate Allen rushed in, scarcely waiting for the rest of the Viking field goal defense. They lined up. Nate blew down the line at the snap of the ball. He flung an arm as the ball came off the kicker's toe and blocked it. Bobby Bryant, sprinting in from the other side, picked up the ball and ran 90 yards to score. Rather sedately, he turned around, alone in the end zone, and blew a kiss to his wife in the bleachers 120 yards away.

Later, on the bench, Nate Allen smiled approvingly. "The Junkman," he said, "strikes again."

Football players know the thin line between being acclaimed as supermen or derided as choke-ups in the clutch. The axiom that the best ones always deliver in the crisis is more romantic than accurate. Actually it's a myth. The great ones do come through much of the time, but certainly not always. Not Tom Brady, not Joe Montana, not Jim Brown or Jerry Rice. The reason was explained by the chronically quotable Lou Holtz. As a college coach Holtz won pretty much anywhere. When Notre Dame was winning, somebody asked him how they happened to lose to an underdog. Holtz had the answer. "Hey," he said, "the other guys give scholarships, too."

In ways not always obvious to the audiences and the narrators of pro football, the most candid pictures of its fundamental appeal may come from the players themselves. You can hear it in the times when their walls are down, when they are giddy after winning or morose in defeat; or when they're having fun with some of the clichés and pretensions of the game itself.

Football players rarely have the opportunity—the forum isn't usually available—for a serious expression of what the game means to them emotionally, whether in victory or defeat.

Jeff Siemon was a college star at Stanford, a linebacker with the Vikings and a significant player on the Vikings' Super Bowl teams of the 1970s. He was an athlete both powerful and cerebral, a man of religious faith and strong values as well as competitiveness. During the Vikings' 1976 season, which ended with the Super Bowl defeat, he kept a daily journal with the understanding that we would collaborate in a book to be published the following year by Harper and Row, regardless of the Super Bowl outcome.

Jeff Siemon's journal was conscientious and thorough each step of the way. He allowed himself a full range of feelings, his thoughts as the season progressed, his concern that he and the coaches weren't on the same page on the severity of an injury he carried into the playoffs, his thoughts about his performance, about his teammates, about his love for his wife.

To reach the Super Bowl, the Vikings had to defeat the Los Angeles Rams in the old Metrodome in the freeze of late December. It wasn't super cold in the Minnesota tradition, but it was cold enough, and the Rams had worked themselves into a fever of intensity remembering their previous failures in the Minnesota cold. One of the major stories of the week was Jeff Siemon's physical condition, and whether he would be of much value because of it. His backup, Amos Martin, opened the game at middle linebacker and Jeff's role early in the game was confined to action with the special teams.

He wrote after the game:

Sunday, December 26 We were leading, 10-0, but the Rams had shown a lot of power on the ground. I noticed on the punting team that my leg was relatively strong. As I was standing on the sideline near Bud Grant I leaned over and said, "Bud, there's no way for me to know whether I can play unless I get in there and try to do something." He nodded and said he would talk to Neill Armstrong, the defensive coach. He suggested that if the Rams made another first down I should go in. They did, and I went in.

I guess every football player has an ego big enough to appreciate special attention. When I heard the fans shouting and applauding as I entered, I was stunned. It was one of the few times I had ever experienced a crowd's reaction to me personally in all my years in football. I knew their reaction was a positive thing that was directed toward me and not against Amos (Martin), who had played well. And I got lucky. Mostly because I wasn't blocked very well, I made a couple of very visible tackles in the first series I was in. I could have been coldly analytical and told myself that it was pure chance, making those tackles. But you're human. You get caught up in the emotion. It's a terrific feeling to actually be part of a championship team.

We didn't stop them every play by a long shot. The Rams are an immensely tough football team. I thought we had established supremacy with Chuck Foreman's 62-yard run and the subsequent touchdown for a 17-0 score. I can chide myself now for saying the Rams were pampered. I don't know whether they are. But they came back with great courage in the second half. And it all came down to that fourth and ten play on our 39 with three minutes to go.

I went over to the sideline to discuss it with Neill Armstrong. It got to whether we would use a four-man rush and our basic defense in that situation or blitz the two outside linebackers. Neill asked me what I'd like to do and I said it was his decision. He said he was leaning toward the blitz, and I said why not, it's a big-play call. Either you do it successfully or you lose the game. I thought it was the kind of hang-it-out call we needed. If the Rams made a first down, they had plenty of time to score; and if we blitzed, there was a real chance they were going to get it all on that play.

The blitz made Pat Haden throw in a hurry. He got it out there, but with just enough loft so that Bobby Bryant was able to make a tremendous play to intercept. I guess you have to be a professional football player to appreciate what he did. When you're one-on-one against a great receiver like Harold Jackson, that is your play. Jackson is all you're supposed to be thinking about. But Bryant had one eye on Jackson and one eye on the quarterback. He's one of the finest big-play football players I've ever seen. He's a ball player who creates the situation for a big play. So he barrelled over as soon as he saw Haden release the ball to Ron Jessie. And then he had to time his jump. I don't think most of the crowd or the television audience really recognized all of the experience, the finesse, the timing and the guts that went into making a play like that.

And then, a few minutes later, there was Tarkenton, who had been struggling all day like most of us—well, it just wasn't one of his better games. But on the one down when all of his skills and mental toughness were needed most, he delivered. That ball he threw to Foreman after seeing his first three receivers covered was one of the greatest clutch passes he or any other quarterback will throw. I spent some time with him in the training room during the week. I know his leg wasn't sound, and it had to affect his maneuverability and therefore his passing performance. But he had that ball right on Foreman's hands on third down-and never mind the windchill factor.

I had a little time to reflect after the game when the mob scene in the dressing room had subsided. I think the closeness you build with your teammates, the sharing of the struggle and those unforgettable flights of jubilation forty-three people take together in victory—or the despondency they shoulder together in defeat—those are the things that make playing worthwhile, in an enduring sense.

145

The belief; the oneness, even if it may be transitory.

I looked over to Carl Eller's locker, where Moose was slowly putting on his tie. I don't know anybody who can make the kind of long-term production out of knotting a tie that Moose can. And I don't know many people—any, really—that I respect more on this team.

In the Rams game, while a lot of people played well (including the Rams, of course), Bobby Bryant and Carl Eller were the guys for the Vikings. Moose was everywhere making tackles. I have played with him for five years, and I can't think of a game where he was better. And here was Carl Eller, twelve years in the league, after absorbing the criticism he did during the season. Yet he was capable in a team crisis of producing a game like that. He had played on the same level the week before, in the playoff game with Washington. What was it Bud said about Moose? When his opponent is good enough or the game is big enough, Eller will give it his undivided attention.

I know it's true. He played the same kind of game last year in the playoffs against Dallas. I think he made ten tackles and three quarterback sacks on Roger Staubach—against one of the finest offensive linemen in modern pro history, Rayfield Wright.

I just wanted to go over to Moose, shake his hand, and tell him how proud I was to be playing with him on the Minnesota Vikings"

(There Jeff's journal passage ends.)

On that day they nearly lost a few getting to the locker room. The stadium regiments charged onto the field from the grandstands by the hundreds in their snowmobile suits, engulfing the players and ambushing the goalposts.

"If we had to play our fans all afternoon instead of the Rams," a shaken Ed White said afterward, "we might not have made it. Coming off the field was like fighting your way through a thousand linebackers. We won the war and nearly got killed enjoying the peace. It was beautiful, but it was brutal. You can't blame the fans for wanting to celebrate, but I wish they would have done it in the parking lot. It wasn't beating on our heads that bothered the ball players. It was their breath that almost knocked us over."

Maybe they should have started some of the fans against Oakland two weeks later.

But that supreme unity and euphoria, during and after one of the biggest games of their lives, in the frosted gloaming at the old Met, was real—and cannot be forgotten by any of the players who felt it.

Yet the unchanging reality for a professional ball player is that if there are winners their inevitably are losers.

No one dealt then with the trials of playing on a chronic loser with the buoyancy of John Campbell, a linebacker from Wadena, MN., who began with a winner—the University of Minnesota teams of the early 1960s, and entered the National Football League with lively expectations. He was totally unprepared for what he found.

Although he began his career with the Vikings, Campbell's memoir describes his years with the impoverished and somewhat renegade Pittsburgh Steelers of the later 1960s. Following his football career Campbell made some major changes in his commitments and values, accepted God and has been involved in an informal ministry and chaplaincy ever since.

But in the 1960s he was a linebacker, and a good one. He also had a receptive eye for the hilarities of life on a losing pro football team. The Steelers today are perennial contenders and six-time Super Bowl champions. During the 1960s, they were considered to be the one team in the NFL committed to a policy of de-emphasizing football.

"That is a libel,' John Campbell said later. "I do think it's fair to say that the Steelers were the only team in the league to go through a whole training camp season without winning an intra-squad game."

John Campbell spent two years with Van Brocklin's Vikings and four with the Steelers of the 1960s. There are few if any living people qualified to wear that combination of campaign ribbons. The Steelers didn't win many games. They actually didn't make many first downs. The most exciting thing the Steelers did offensively was to kick extra points, exciting because suspense would always clutch the Steeler fans: Does Booth Lustig kick the ball this time or does he kick the holder. That actually happened.

In those years the Steelers seemed to constitute their own league. It seemed fairly clear that they didn't belong in the other. Seldom was mediocrity pursued with such fortitude and ingenuity. And yet John Campbell's remembrance of playing with that clan of roustabouts and vaudevillians is warm, deep and, well, forgiving.

I have to tell you [he said] *the Steelers came out of some unknown time zone. We played a game in Cleveland on Saturday night where they introduced the teams before 80,000 people. You ran across the baseball diamond onto the field. They introduced Preston Carpenter of our group. He came sailing out of the runway, rounded first and slid into second with the prettiest hook slide they ever saw in Cleveland. He got up, dusted himself off and doffed his helmet to the crowd, which roared and screamed for him to steal third.*

The Steelers were the last great collection of bar-fighting football players to survive both curfew and municipal court. The only thing we didn't do was pass the hat during the game. It was that type of outfit. Anytime you put Bobby Layne, the ornery quarterback, on the staff with Buddy Parker, the coach, you are going to have problems. The guys would sit there and fight. Or they'd stand there and fight, and then they'd go out and have drinks together. You would see one of your teammates come back and his face would look like nine miles of bad road, and he'd been in a fight with one of his buddies over some girl in Rhode Island.

You can't believe the pep talk Parker gave us one game. We were playing the 49ers at Brown University. It's an exhibition, on national television. Parker is standing there, taking down half a cigarette in one drag, putting his nose in the fork of fingers when he inhaled the cigarette, the classic Parker style. He is looking around the locker room and you can see he's trying to figure out a way to trade the whole team. And he says, 'Okay, I want you to see if you can go out there for all of your millions of TV fans without tripping over your feet.'

That was it. That was the pep talk. I looked at Charlie Bradshaw, and I said, 'I don't know when I've been this stirred up about a game.'

We went out and they just buried us. They fired Parker a few hours later, just before he was about to get rid of all 40 ballplayers.

I mentioned Charlie Bradshaw—a great, decent guy. He must have gone 6 foot 9 and 250. But he always used to have this clean uniform. He said he wasn't helping anybody rolling around in the mud. A couple of the guys didn't see that because they figure you got to be grubby-looking to play well. But Charlie had the right idea. We used to call him Mr. Clean or The White Rabbit. He was in the bar one day drinking buttermilk and this guy comes in and says, 'Hey Charlie, how you doing?' and knocks over his buttermilk. Charlie ordered another one. The guy comes back a few minutes later on his way from the men's room and says, 'Well, I see you're still on the stuff,' and he knocks over Charlie's buttermilk again.

Charlie didn't say a word. He just picked the guy up and threw him out the window. I don't mean he threw him out the open window. I mean he threw him through the WINDOW. The first thing the guy hit was a fire hydrant and the last we heard about him he was assigned to Ward 3.

It didn't take much of an excuse to start a celebration with the Steelers. I remember one year we opened the season by kicking off to the Chicago Bears. The guy caught the ball five yards deep in the end zone. That was good, but the bad part was that the guy was Gale Sayers. Eleven seconds later the score is 7-0.

One minute later Bill Nelson is going to execute our first play and throws the ball with great velocity and character. Unfortunately it went to the Chicago cornerback. It is now 14-0 and our defense has not been on the field yet. But would you believe we won the game 41-13? And the next week we tied the Giants. And so we all went down to the Roosevelt Hotel to celebrate afterward.

Hundreds of fans were down there and you'd swear we'd won the Super Bowl.

It was as close as we got to the Super Bowl. We lost the next nine in a row.

Pittsburgh then actually was a great place to play if you wanted to save money. The Steelers paid average salaries under lovable Art Rooney but when I was there you were so ill thought-of that you never went out for dinner. You couldn't. You could go to the nicest place in Pittsburgh. People would recognize you as a Steeler and they would come over and start yelling at you. It's the truth.

They tried in those years to make a character out of the knuckleball kicker, Booth Lustig. This was too bad, because none of the things they invented about Boots were half as astonishing as the truth. Boots' ball behaved mysteriously. He is still the only placement kicker in the history of the NFL who kicked a conversion try that went OVER the line of scrimmage and UNDER the goalposts. I mean the ball was higher when it past the line of scrimmage than it was when it past the goal line two yards further.

He used to start kicking paper cups for practice as soon as our offense got the ball…He actually kicked the paper cups farther than the football.

He broke up our practice one day and almost turned Ray Mansfield, a fine center, into a soprano. Ray snapped the ball for a field goal attempt, and Dick Hoak—a really great holder—put the ball down. Boots gave it a heckuva shot and kicked the ball right into Mansfield's bottom.

You can imagine the position Mansfield was in, all stretched out like that after just centering the ball. Poor Ray just went down like he took a mortar shot. The whole team was helpless, flopping around the ground laughing, and they carried poor Ray into the locker room.

The next week Boots kicked Dick Hoak in the hand.

He just missed the ball completely and hit Hoak square in

the knuckles. They said it couldn't be done, but Boots did it.

Boots had this little blue flight bag in which he carried his shoes. He wore different kinds of shoes for different kicks. Maybe they should have left Boots alone and examined the shoes. We were playing the Eagles, and it had to be the worst pro football game ever played, which is a statement I do not make lightly. That was the famed O. J. Simpson Bowl, in which the loser would get draft rights to O. J.

Everybody was cheering for us to lose. The Steelers rose to the occasion brilliantly and won the game, 6-3 destroying any chance we had of getting Simpson. As it turned out, Buffalo was even worse than the Eagles or the Steelers and they drafted him. But that was the game when Boots put it all together. He had some early discouragements. He missed field goals of 10 and 11 yards (the posts were on the goal line in those years) and a real toughie of 15 yards - which was right in the middle of the field. The others were off to the side. But with just 10 seconds left and the score tied, in comes Boots. The ball is at the 25, and he puts it through.

The guys unanimously gave Boots the game ball. It was a tremendous honor because game balls were very rarely given when I was with the Steelers. I mean they were really collector's items. For a while the players debated whether we should give Boots a paper cup instead of a ball.

But fate, as they say, is no respecter of the mighty. We played a game in Buffalo and got beat by one point. Boots missed a field goal or extra point or some such thing. He felt so bad that he wouldn't even go back on the plane with the team. He grabbed his bags, took a cab and went on the highway hitchhiking.

And wouldn't you know the guys who picked him up were Buffalo fans, and when they found out who he was they invited him to leave the car. I asked the people in Buffalo about it and they said it happened exactly that way.

A few years after John Campbell and most of his teammates

retired, the Steelers drafted a quarterback named Terry Bradshaw. They acquired a lineman named Mean Joe Greene, receivers named Lynn Swann and John Stallworth, linebackers named Jack Lambert and Jack Hamm, and a running back named Franco Harris. Pittsburgh won the first four of its six Super Bowls with this crew, and Boots Lustig was forgotten—but not quite by all.

"Nobody who played with Boots can possibly forget him," John Campbell.

No. 1 in their hearts. Unfortunately, last in field goals.

13

The Lonely Crusade of Matt Birk

The NFL's college draft in 1998 dragged into its groggy hours. The early rounds were over and the usual roll call of late-round obscurities was relayed to the dozing audiences. The routine was punctuated by some off-stage snickers when the Minnesota Vikings announced, as their sixth round selection—and the draft's 173rd player chosen—a lineman about to graduate in economics at Harvard.

One of the draftniks in the audience rolled his eyes. "This pick HAS to be a little different," he said. At the time, no one guessed how different.

Matt Birk began by upending the laws of chance and making the Vikings' roster. In two years he was playing in the Pro Bowl and doing it annually as one of the best centers and offensive linemen in professional football. He was an Ivy Leaguer but also a 260-pounder conditioned to the savage muscle wars on the line of scrimmage.

He was more. He was a moderating voice in the locker room during the years of Randy Moss and related tempests. He was a popular figure with the Viking public, a community leader who involved himself with underprivileged kids, building playgrounds and creating recognition for high achieving students. For the last few years he poured his energy and money into a movement to divert a small percentage of pro football's largesse into making life easier for old-time football players, many of them hospital cases who had missed out on football's windfall and the pensions players receive today. Birk's was basically a thankless mission that attracted few recruits among his playing peers around the league. But he did not abandon it and he remained a fixture on the Minnesota sporting landscape.

Yet in the winter of 2009, he left the Vikings to sign a multi-million dollar three-year contract with the Baltimore Ravens, who welcomed him with hugs and balloons.

The explanations, both from the Vikings and from Birk himself, were polite but obscure. He had been looking for a strong signal from the Vikings that he was wanted back for a 12th season. Such signals usually involve money and contract extensions. None appeared. The Vikings didn't seem distraught when he left, and the unspoken signal probably had something to do with the Vikings' conviction that Matt Birk's' best years were gone and the team had to move on.

But whatever the merit of either decision, Birk's or the Vikings, this is an athlete of substance without flash, one whose perceptions of the game he plays are revealing and yet rarely inflammatory. In short, this is a well-adjusted guy who loves his game, knows most of the secrets of that strange and chaotic world of the line of scrimmage in pro football, and manages to emerge from it with not only a professional ethic but social conscience.

Players thrust into that ultimate war zone of pro football's scrimmage line seldom give you graphic, hair-turning accounts of the routine violence of that kind of life. The people who run, throw and catch the ball are usually more prolific talkers. Ironically, Matt Birk found open arms for his services in Baltimore after the 2008 season because the Ravens' center, Jason Brown, had signed a juicy contract with the St. Louis Rams after Baltimore was eliminated in the playoffs. And it was Brown who had gone public a few weeks earlier with a few horror stories of life on the line of scrimmage in pro football. Some of those stories can be grim and sometimes they are hilarious, but it IS another world.

It's one that is not very well policed, Jason Brown told the NFL's Sirius radio and later William Rhoden of the *New York Times*.

"We have to prepare ourselves to actually dislike, to the point of almost hating, our opponents," he said. He told of the punching and grappling in the scrimmage pileups and suggested that the officials were often caught in a dilemma. They couldn't call all the penalties and had little choice but to allow some of the caveman behavior that defines life in football's trenches. It's a world where even TV cameras have a hard time penetrating. It often comes down to three-feet of frozen grass contested by huge and ferocious men, clawing and pounding at each other with a fury and desperation that obscures the fact that a good percentage of them are multi-millionaires.

From Steeler coach Mike Tomlin, the Super Bowl champion, came this order of battle: "Our goal is to impose our will on the other team."

It does sound medieval, which may not be all that far from the truth. Yes, there are those lovely arching spirals of the accomplished quarterback, and the silken body control of receivers like Larry Fitzgerald in his leaping catches; there is the manic energy of Troy Palamalu. Adrian Peterson stirs the adrenalin of the arena thousands with sudden shifts of speed and direction that launch him toward the end zone whether 10 or 80 yards away.

But the battle is usually won by overweight grunts who whale at each other on the line of scrimmage. This is said in no derision. These people are athletes in ways not covered by the lofty language draped on the pass-receiving gazelles. But they do play closer to the ground and they're usually the guys who are publicly branded as the ball game's cheaters: The referee pronounces the verdict: "Holding, offense, No. 75. Ten yards." It's usually the only time their numbers draw attention.

Well, sure, No. 75 was guilty and he did hold. If he didn't, the pass rusher was going to break his quarterback's neck.

Sometimes a dark comedy evolves from those Neanderthal scenes deep in the scrimmage pile. In the late 1960s, Conrad Dobler, an offensive lineman who played for the St. Louis Cardinals, established himself as the reigning carnivore of the National Football League. His behavior was chronicled professionally but bluntly by a Viking defensive tackle named Doug Sutherland. Sutherland was a strong and reliable football player not normally given to hyperbole.

"The guy bit me," Sutherland reported after a Viking-Cardinal game in St. Louis. "Nobody ever bit me before in a football game.

Matt Birk's 11 years with the Vikings were marked by all-pro seasons, community service, and efforts to bring aid to old time players left out of football's prosperity.

Right there in the calf. It was under the pile. I yelled to the official." The official evidently wasn't equipped with x-ray vision. Dobler, who was actually a good football player, denied all charges. He implied that his mother didn't raise him to be a vampire. He said Sutherland had to be a little squirrely to make a charge like that. "I'm aggressive, true," Dobler said. "But why would I be biting people? First off, it sounds awfully unsanitary."

He also charged that Sutherland was no Little Boy Blue under the pile himself. There were other reports around the league, however, that Dobler was a thoroughly nasty man in those pileups, and it got to the point where the next time they met Sutherland threatened to wear catcher's shin pads if Dobler was in the lineup. The feud ended before any rabies tests were required.

With 11 years in pro football, Matt Birk obviously is aware of this kind of turmoil on the line of scrimmage, and he didn't argue with Jason Brown's description. "When you see those defensive linemen and linebackers coming wild with fire in their eyes," he said, "I suppose you could call it a little barbaric."

But he had the sound of man who accepted that as a line of business in a game where the make-believe war is being waged by a lot of people who have earned millions, including Matt Birk.

So what's a guy like Birk doing in all of this, from the Ivy League, of all places, with a degree in economics?

Nobody who arrived on the Vikings' roster from such a remote throw of the dice has rewarded his employers more prodigally. Birk contributed that same high level of professionalism year after year. Nor have there been many players with the same recognition of a larger world of human need beyond the gates of the arena. Birk took up the challenge to bring some relief and opportunity to the disadvantaged with the same resolve he exhibited on the field, enlisting his prominence as a football player to attract support.

He brought to that wider world one other dimension: his own gratitude.

Birk grew up playing kid football in St. Paul, then in high school, without thinking seriously about football beyond—until his high school coach said: "You can play college football." And Matt Birk decided that Harvard would be a good place to find out.

The National Football League is not congested with Ivy League graduates. But Birk learned to appreciate the game at Harvard in an atmosphere of growth on campus and in the classroom. He played it well and made the Vikings' roster as a rookie in 1998. By his third season he had established himself as the regular center, one of the team's best players in an offense that averaged nearly 400 yards a game. With quarterback Daunte Culpepper he went to the Pro Bowl early in his career, then annually, and he also earned what might have been an even more exclusive post-season award, the All-Madden team made up of players John Madden calls "the true gamers."

It got to be predictable, the post-season honors for Matt Birk, but somewhere along the way he began thinking of another side to the high visibility he had reached as a pro football star. It wasn't exactly an epiphany. Birk carried into his professional career some important values he acquired at home and in his adolescence. As his profile grew in the community, he remembered. "You know, I felt blessed to have gotten where I am. I looked back and remembered all of the teachers, coaches, parents and neighbors who helped me. A lot of them went out of their way. Some of those people took a lot of time. They didn't have to do it. They weren't getting any reward for taking five minutes to do this or 30 minutes to do that, or even days to do it. But some of those things make us what we become. I feel good about talking to kids, and I know a lot of them look up to football players, or any adults who are willing to take time with them. Hey, most kids think adults are pretty cool. A lot of people don't realize that. It matters especially if some of those kids aren't getting enough attention at home. You can talk to them. If you have the time and it's the place, you should talk to them."

With a growing family of his own, he organized a foundation to honor deserving high school students and called it HIKE, for Hope, Inspiration, Knowledge and Education. He built other civic groups committed to lifting up the less fortunate and has become a kind of large and genial minstrel in the community, reminding it that none of us makes it on our own, and some need that lift desperately. But in the last two years he has become most visible, when he's not on the line of scrimmage, appealing to his peers in pro football to consider the hard conditions of life for many of the men who pioneered the game or played it when the salaries had not yet reached the level of a living wage.

Some of those old-timers are broken in health, with little or no money. They may have had opportunities, maybe not. Some of them went for the booze. Many of them lived ordinary lives afterward, and watched pro football acquire ever greater levels of public frenzy and revenue. But a lot of them got hurt playing the game before there was a pension plan or adequate medical attention.

"After I'd moved into my career in pro football," Birk said, "I began thinking about the guys who made it possible. There was a story here and there about a retired player who'd come on hard times. I knew there'd been attempts in the past to get them covered in the league agreements with the players. I know there have been hard feelings about that, and growing up I remember NFL players walking the picket lines during the strike back in 1987. By the time I entered pro ball in 1998, of course, the money we were making had gotten much larger. The National Football League had really taken off. As a player you always think about life after football. You're always one serious injury away from being out of it. When you're younger you feel so strong, sort of invincible, that you can sometimes take things for granted. But when football is over now, we have benefits that the pioneers in this league didn't have. I've met some of them, and I did feel that they'd more or less been forgotten. Some of them were in dire need. Still trying to deal with injuries. Some aren't able to work. Some of them actually needed a place to live."

There's contention in the National Football League and among some of its players about how to meet this obligation—or if, in fact, an obligation even exists. The Players Association opposed the attempt by retired players to expand the union's disability program, arguing that the union's primary responsibility is to its active members. The struggle put Birk and the union's leadership on opposing sides.

People like Birk, Kyle Turley, and former coach Mike Ditka, among others, believe that pro football has a moral responsibility to an older generation of players who missed out on the payoff and health benefits in a game they helped popularize. To dramatize the need, Birk and others organized the non-profit Gridiron Greats to build awareness around the country and to recruit donors. The response included a million dollar donation from the Laser Spine Institute of Florida and Arizona. Birk put $75,000 of his own money into the organization, and he is the organization's most visible spokesman today, though he admits the battle is uphill.

There has been no overwhelming rush among today's players to respond to Birk's appeal. In the first few weeks prior to the 2009 Super Bowl—where Birk was one of the finalists in the NFL's Man of the Year award—less than 1 per cent of the National Football League players gave money.

Birk's reaction is measured. He made no judgments but he said he wasn't going to be deterred. Ditka was less measured. "What's that tell you?" he said. "Would you call that apathy?"

"The toll of playing football," Birk said, "has left some of our brothers physically unable to work. Many of them did not play when the salaries and benefits were anywhere close to what they are today. Sadly, the price paid by some of those who came before us has been too costly. They live in excruciating pain and severe mental anguish as a direct result from their playing days."

A *Minneapolis Star Tribune* reporter asked sympathetically what prompted him to risk unpopularity with some of his peers by crusading for old and forgotten players who took their chances when the game was still struggling.

"I get asked that all the time," he said. "To me, that's the silliest question in the world. Why wouldn't I get involved?"

In other words, "If not us, who?"

Coincidentally, the *Star Tribune*'s Rachel Blount reported on the findings of another organization that has been a kind of watchdog over the apparent rise in significant injuries in major contact sports. The Sports Legacy Institute revealed what it said was new evidence that NFL players are at risk of developing serious brain damage from the effects of repeated head trauma.

Head trauma is another word for concussions which, with the use of the helmet as a battering ram, intentionally or not, has become a major concern in the National Football League.

"In one sense, this hardly seems news," she said. "With ever bigger, faster players crashing into each other Sunday after Sunday, with fans clamoring for tooth-rattling hits they can replay on You Tube, semi-regulated violence remains the cornerstone of football's allure." The story quoted Chris Nowinski, the president of Sports Legacy.

"People are not taking this seriously enough by a long shot," he said. "Active players don't want to talk about it. They have a short window of time to make money in the game, and they don't want to think what happens to the brain when they run into a 300-pound man at 20 miles an hour. And the NFL's research is borderline pathetic. Our ultimate goal would be for nobody to develop CTE (chronic traumatic encephalopathy or brain disease) Our initial goal is just to give people a choice. Nobody knew that multiple concussions would lead to this."

The condition he's talking about is commonly associated with the image of punch-drunk boxers, groping with reality. It may be a condition routinely described as dementia or Alzheimer's among older people. But Nowinski contends that among former athletes the symptoms might just as well—and possibly more accurately—be described as the CTE, a condition once associated primarily with ex-boxers.

This perspective sheds a different and less attractive light on a game that thrives on the spectacle of powerful athletes battering one another with unparalleled force.

And it's not that the pro game's authorities don't recognize a hazard. Penalties are frequently called against pass rushers for using their helmets in attacking the quarterback, and against tacklers who spear their opponents with their helmets. But many players themselves are infuriated by tougher rules because, as we so frequently are reminded, "This is a game of contact. Let the players play." The pass rushers want the sacks. It means more money.

Birk's is not the first attempt to remind football of its past, and of the plight of some of the players of that era who became victims of inadequate medical attention or skimpy wages. He hardly qualifies as a noisy rebel battling the institution. He's a ballplayer, husband, father and a full-ranging explorer of the good life and camaraderie that football has brought to him. But he also has a conscience that tells him something ought to be done.

The offensive lineman once was an obscurity in football. In today's TV saturation, there are no obscurities. Some of those obscurities are drawing $6 and $7 million a year. But offensive lineman have a different slant on the game from their heavyweights facing them across the line of scrimmage.

John Michels, the coach of the great Viking offensive lines of Ron Yary, Ed White and Mick Tinglehoff, used to talk about it. "The defensive lineman, the big tackles and the pass rushers, are actually the attackers on the line of scrimmage," he said. "The offensive guys have the job of stopping them or slowing them down. So the dynamics of the game force them to play a passive game compared with the guys on the other side. Sometimes you'll actually have guys on the offensive line who work themselves into a disposition or personality that reflects that."

A kind of private militancy, an indrawn personality?

Seething resentment?

Michels would smile at that. "For the defensive rusher, it's bombs away. The offensive lineman often has to be smarter, quieter and mentally tougher."

Which doesn't mean the offensive lineman is going to be bashful when the collisions come. Matt Birk doesn't give the impression of being very passive. But he does agree with White, who has commented about the compensating stages or moments in a football game that put the job of line blocking on the edge of actual euphoria.

"When you get a drive going down the field," White said, "and you're getting 5 and 6 yards on every running play, you can't wait to get back in the huddle. And you'd hear guys saying, 'Run it again.' That was the real high of playing football. You were on a roll, you were knocking them backwards and you were together and you wanted to say, 'The hell with throwing. Let's keep running.'"

Birk knows the feeling. "It's a little different game today, of course," he said. "It's opened up more with more variations on offense. But, he's right. The camaraderie for the lineman is at its height when you're rolling like that.

"I understand what Ed White was saying. You do get caught up in the momentum of a long drive like that, and the solidarity you feel. It still happens. We had a pretty incredible drive like that going in a game with Carolina. We were moving, every down. It went for 22 plays and ate up most of the quarter."

"And what happened?"

"We got a field goal out of it."

A little bit of bathos never hurt anyone. The Vikings won the game.

Nobody plays in the meat grinder of the line of scrimmage in pro football for 11 years without paying the physical price, feeling the emotional pain of defeat on the brink of the euphoria. Birk played on the special teams in his rookie 1998 season, when the Vikings lost a shot at the Super Bowl on a missed 38-yard field goal in the conference championship game. He missed all of the 2005 season with serious hip injury and sports hernia.

But he had the sound of a man who accepted that as part of the bargain in a game where the make-believe war is waged by a lot of people who have made millions, including Matt Birk.

Is it earned?

The ball players are going to be the first to tell you, "It is, royally."

And because Birk knows there were hundreds of other guys years ago who went through that same rigor and mauling, and now can't live a decent life, he keeps his fund drive going in hopes of lifting the others out of oblivion.

He hadn't heard much about a romantic football figure out of another time, Johnny Blood, one of the most improbable personalities to figure in the nearly 100 years of pro football. He was the man who preceded Matt Birk in calling on the conscience of today's football heroes.

But some of us knew him well, Johnny Blood McNally. You'll find his name and his bust in Canton in the Hall of Fame Museum. In fact, as a voting member of the Hall of Fame selection committee in the 1960s, I voted for him. He was elected on merit, although he probably deserved it for a variety of reasons only loosely connected with football. He played with several teams in the NFL of the late 1920s and early '30s, among them the Green Bay Packers. He was a running back, a defensive back, an extraordinary punter and pretty much a football prodigy.

They did have trouble finding him nights before the games, or on any particular night. John McNally was a boulevardier of pro football's barnstorming, high-shoe, leather helmet times. He played football at St. John's University in Minnesota. Although his family had money, college ball wasn't enough and he picked up side money playing for semi-pro teams whenever they came through or wherever he could find them. He played well, often and for hire. This was slightly in violation of the college rules and the amateur status of their football, of course, but John was resourceful. Walking downtown one night he looked up at the theater marquee and saw the movie title, *Blood and Sand* with Rudolf Valentino, the ranking film lover of the era. "That's it," he told his buddy. "I think I'll call myself Johnny Blood." Which he became. The name was too good to abandon when he became a pro football player. John never regarded himself as serious competition for Valentino in the field of itinerant romance, but he wasn't any palooka, either.

What he was, from end to end of notable but relatively brief career, was a rascal and a roamer. He'd arrive for afternoon practice 30 minutes after ending a jolly night with two hours of sleep. When the coach sent an assistant to track him down to face the music one day, he slipped out of his hotel room and hung by his fingers on the brick ledge of an eighth floor window until the danger was past.

In later years he taught economics and literature as a college professor. He was a remarkably handsome man with perfectly coiffed white hair that made him a dramatic figure at some of the league reunions. One of the last times I saw him, John had imbibed generously during the cocktail hour. I overhead him reciting Shelley behind the palm fronds of the lobby of the old Northland Hotel in Green Bay.

But in his last years John struggled seriously to bring some share of football's burgeoning prosperity to the older players of the '20s and '30s, some of whom had suffered severely during the Great Depression. He made no headway. His last proposal urged the NFL to create a best-out-of-three Super Bowl, the profits of the second game to go into the retired players pension fund. The league sighed. THREE SUPER BOWL GAMES!!!

We don't know. They may reconsider.

John was an unchained spirit in those years that verged on hobo football. But he was also a perceptive guy who thought a little deeper about the equities in the game he played. Three Super Bowls are a little much and definitely scary. They could finish two days before the college draft in April.

But he had a cause. So does Matt Birk. So does the National Football League when it starts looking harder into player protection. It did so in its annual meeting in March of 2009, toughening the rules to protect players when they are vulnerable to the use of helmet or to dangerous follow-through roughing. Traditionalists, including some of the players, tended to react unhappily to these new player protections, denouncing them as milquetoast intrusions on a game that is by nature tough and physical. On the other hand, the league might think seriously about a penalty tougher than 15 yards for spearing with the helmet. Eviction might be a start.

14

Ladies Break Down the Lodge Doors

The air exploded with colored confetti and the bedlam of a football crowd delivered from years of ignominy. The Arizona Cardinals had upset Philadelphia to win their first major title in 60 years, lifting them into the Super Bowl. On the field, Fox's sideline reporter, Pam Oliver, pulled the Cardinals' Adrian Wilson out of the chaos of his hugging teammates and the euphoric fans who had spilled out of the Phoenix stadium.

Adrian Wilson, a defensive back, was not the star of the game. Larry Fitzgerald had caught three touchdown passes, and quarterback Kurt Warner brought the Cardinals back from the grave—after they had squandered an 18-point lead—by throwing one more touchdown pass in the final minutes. Fitzgerald and Warner might not have been available to Pam Oliver in that celebrating frenzy after the game. In the sports reporting business, it happens all the time. Hands clutching microphones are grabbing for the stars, sometimes pushing other hands away. It can be a real rugby scrum.

Women reporters are now part of that action, after years in which they were marginalized or dismissed as part of the gender outreach. The ones we see on television, and many we don't, are generally first rate and serious professionals—Pam Oliver, Michele Tafoya, and many others.

I don't think it was easy for Pam Oliver that day. Any producer will want you to "get" the star or stars of a momentous game like this, with its huge television audience.

So here were Pam Oliver and Adrian Wilson, who shared an

ethnic heritage, on camera a day before the Martin Luther King holiday and two days before Barack Obama became the first African American president. He was the Cardinals' senior player, on the roster for eight years, a time of almost unrelieved ridicule and tumult. For Wilson and the rest it had been loss after loss. They were the dregs of the league. There had been a conga line of coaching changes, trades that boomeranged, and the eventual shrugging disgust of the public. The team was a doormat and it wasn't going to change.

And now, the team, Wilson's team, was going to the Super Bowl.

The reporter asked the veteran what this day meant to him.

He answered emotionally but said the expected things about enduring all of the bad times, the team staying together and now this, the ultimate redemption.

He didn't get much beyond that because of the tears he couldn't restrain. He tried to control himself, but it was hard. The reporter lightly placed her hand on his shoulder pads, a small gesture that conveyed understanding.

A little unprofessional?

No, I wouldn't call it that.

After all those years of ignominy Adrian Wilson's team was a champion and he was overcome emotionally in the moment. Pam Oliver was a reporter interviewing him before an audience of millions. They shared a heritage.

You don't generally use language like "graceful" when you talk about football reporters. It can be construed as sexist, I suppose, when it's attributed to a woman. And yet I liked what Pam Oliver did in the less than a minute she had. Beyond that, she is a also a first-rate reporter, an award-winner.

Before the day was over, I was doing some reflecting of my own, not on the coincidences of the game but seeing in later years the dramatically expanding involvement of women as followers of the game, and now the growing role of women reporting it, on television and in the press boxes of print and online journalism. And right about this time I cheerfully remembered the days of our football clinic for women.

It may have traced back to a letter from a reader of the *Minneapolis Star Tribune*. It came from women in the middle of the football season in the 1970s, when color TV had become widespread and pro football's popularity was just beginning to soar. She wrote with the cold fury of a woman betrayed.

You should remember that it was a time when football had begun seriously to horn in on Sunday afternoons, which once were the province of quiet weekends in most of America. At the ballgames the bands still played at halftime but by then the country was beginning to understand the language of pro football; and American women were starting to take sides on the value of having this expanding gorilla—the game, not their husbands—in the living room.

The burden of this woman's message was this: she wasn't opposed to football, but football had now usurped something precious in her household, the weekend hours when she and her husband did things together—a dinner out, a walk, and then some luxurious wrestles in bed; times when they were freed from the stresses of work and of chronically sociable neighbors. Here is close to a verbatim transcript of her letter, mailed from a sizable community in central Minnesota.

"I don't hate football," she said. "I don't even dislike it. I go to all the games. I humor my husband's drunken friends in the parking lot when one of them yells, 'hey, blondie, let's work on our bump-and-run.' I wear those goofy wool tassel caps and sneer when somebody mentions Howard Cosell! I pretend to know the difference between a blitz and banana route—all the orthodox things like that.

"But television football is breaking me down. I'm not thinking about the divorce courts. I think of the convents. I visualize myself as an abbess. It's what football television is doing to me.

"Football and the pros have turned our weekends upside down. Our Saturday nights now are what the Friday nights used to be, the big party night. Only now he parties like a big wheel because he knows so much about the game that he feels like one of the owners. The game is right in the living room, all the time, and he spends the whole party with our friends and neighbors talking about our front four and how some guy has got to have the world's fastest release. It goes on that way for hours. By the time it's over he's all smashed out and worthless for anything but dead ballast."

I admit grieving as I read this letter. I was tempted to telephone, but there was more in the letter.

"Before noon he's got all of the TV lineups from the Sunday sports page spread out on the coffee table. It's not a minute too soon, either, because the commentators are coming on the tube telling us what to look for when Kansas City lines up with its tight end in the "I" instead of the slot. My husband says this confuses the strong safety.

"Isn't that beautiful? The strong safety is confused. What about me? Am I supposed to be panting to find out where the tight end lines up?"

Right there, I decided to call.

"You're feeling neglected because of televised football," I said.

"Typhoid Mary has had better years," she said.

"Have you thought," I said with a great surge of delicacy, "about trying to entice your husband at halftime?"

"I have," she said, "But the sonofabuck likes marching bands, too."

I hung up sympathetically, but with some sense of guilt.

By then, the general acceptance of pro football Sundays was no longer the subject of academic debate in America. But there is no doubt about the general confusion among millions of women about football basics, back in that era when the game was taking off and its arcane language prompted many of them to throw up their hands and exclaim "WHAT is this all about"—blitzes, Hail Marys, tight ends, draw plays—what IS this?

So I went to the newspaper's managing editor with a proposition: We, as public servants and explorers of the human condition, had an obligation to bring the basics of pro football to the women of our community.

The managing editor was not immediately overwhelmed. "Explain to me," he said, "why we have this obligation?"

Pro football I said, was a developing phenomenon. It was Exhibit

A conversationally all over town and throughout America for at least six months running. Sadly this was primarily a one-sided conversation, almost entirely male, but my mail was suggesting that a lot of women wanted to know more about it—not to compete with it for the attention of the men in their life but because they see that this business of football is getting bigger every day. It's a happening and they want to know more about it."

So what do you propose, the managing editor said.

"Let's offer a football clinic for women. Let's run it every other week. We'll make only a nominal charge, $10 for eight sessions, every other Tuesday. We can hold it in some public place that's fairly central. We'll make it fundamental. We do it on a blackboard, line up the Xs and Os by position, and give the responsibilities for each position. We'll talk about the language of the game and try to take a little of the mystery out of it."

The editor folded his arms. "All right, it might be a service after all. And who are you going to bring in to be the instructor."

I looked at him with disappointment. "Well, ah, I think I qualify. I cover the game and know the players. You just don't want too much erudition in this job, do you? Contracting with a coach or former player who would inflate the budget?"

"Certainly not. We don't want an inflated budget. Tell you what. We'll do a little ad for it. If as many as 25 women show up, we'll go for it."

They ran the ad and about 150 women showed up.

There wasn't room for all of them. We moved the sessions from the newspaper's cafeteria to the auditorium of a motel and then to the ballroom of a supper club when the attendance went past 200.

"Learn the difference," one of the ads went, "between a red dog and a hot dog." Once in a while I'd give the scholars a question to try out on their know-everything-about-football husbands. "Ask him innocently this week how far the hash marks are from the sideline."

It was always a mystery to the husband. (All right, you fountain of knowledge in the house, how far ARE the hash marks from the sideline? The answer is on the last page of this chapter) The women beamed. They came back two weeks later to announce their triumph. We'd bring in one of the Vikings as a guest. The big coup one year was to introduce Herschel Walker a half hour after he got off the plane in the big trade with Dallas. Secretaries, homemakers, pensioners and wealthy suburbanites attended. We gave a quiz after the seventh session, 20 questions, the last one was an essay type with a limit of 20 words. Something like "Define the shotgun formation." I was the professor, grading each paper. Nobody flunked. We'd have sessions dissecting the tactics and strategy of the four-man pass rush and the safety blitz.

On graduation night I would show up in an academic gown, one of them borrowed from the president of Augsburg College in Minneapolis. Each of the students was awarded a diploma. The Viking coach was the commencement speaker. Fundamentally, the coaches loved it—Bud Grant, Jerry Burns, Denny Green. It was strictly Q and A and no stress for the coaches. Everybody adored them, of course. One year the Viking coach couldn't make it. I telephoned Lou Holtz, then the University of Minnesota coach, probably the highest priced speaker among all of the college coaches. At the graduation he spoke for 50 minutes and the scholars couldn't get enough of it. When it was over I offered Holtz the usual honorarium, something in three figures. "You know, " he said, "this has been so great I want you to give that money to any cause these women want."

We took a vote and named a deserving charity and Holtz insisted on coming back the next year if possible. It wasn't. He was coaching Notre Dame the next year.

Clearly, such an aroused student body needed the added academic experience of a field trip. And so we had them annually, usually to Chicago for the Vikings-Bears game at Soldier Field or Vikings-Green Bay at Lambeau. Even for the Green Bay excursion, though, we always stayed at the old Bismarck Hotel in downtown Chicago. The old Bismarck seemed to have a suitably academic ambience, with ivy creeping in on the entrance. We chartered a bus, sometimes two, sometimes three and arrived Friday evenings. The entourage got that big because occasionally husbands or boyfriends were invited. The women, I regret to say, were as much fans as they were students and they would come into the stadium wearing their purple and yellow Viking regalia—long Brunhilde braids and horned helmets. I told them above all not to get into arguments in the stadium with the Chicago crowd. The Bears' fans—not the most genteel in the National Football League—recognized my flock at the start of each game by pouring beer on their heads.

Naturally, I took exception to this affront. The Brunhildes took even greater exception and prepared to throw mustard-slathered hot dogs in the faces of the locals. I considered this bad strategy because the Bears had us outnumbered by about 60,000 to 210. Oddly, the Bears' fans were humbled by the adult attitude on the part of the more mannered Minnesotans and eventually invited them to their tailgate parties after the games—prompting all hands to claim one more small triumph for the virtues of reconciliation.

This didn't help much the year we issued the popular little two-foot inflatable Viking swords that the team sold as souvenirs.

On Saturday nights before game day I usually enlisted the group buses to ferry the scholars from the hotel to Rush St., the entertainment magnet of downtown Chicago. Strategically I got lost as quickly as possible after the women fanned out on Rush, and I returned to the hotel to bask in the joys of peace and quiet.

A few minutes before midnight I got a call from a restaurant bar. It was hard to make out the caller's message, all but drowned out by noisy conversation and general turmoil. The caller talked louder. "You got some kind of group of women football fans here from Minneapolis?" he asked.

Flags of danger immediately went up in my head. "Why do you want to know?" I asked.

He described the scene. I said yes and no, I was in charge of more than 200 knowledge-craving women from my football clinic. In no way, I said, could this be described as a group.

"The women are individualists," I said. "They're pursuing independent study."

The voice at the bar grunted without approval. I tried to put a face on this man and mentally thumbed through the old post office bulletin boards that publicized the rap sheets of fugitives from justice. It didn't help. I pictured an old pirate galleymaster with folded earrings and pointed ears.

"The one I'm looking at ain't pursuing independent study," he said. "She's got this crazy rubber sword and she's trying to attack my customers like she's a matador. It's worse than that. She's got five others with her who are doing the same thing. She said you taught them how to go hut-hut-hut like a quarterback. I told her to take her act back to the Halloween party, but she said they mean no harm and they were just getting psyched up for the game and she gave me your name and your hotel."

I asked him if it was the woman with the purple caterpillar antennae. He said he couldn't pick her out. "But I'll tell you this. If that one comes through the door the one I'm talking to goes out the window."

And then he got really menacing.

"I'm telling you pal, if she drills somebody with the goofy little sword, you're an accessory."

I told him to do nothing until I got there.

A half hour later we all left the place more or less intact and without handcuffs.

Call it the price of scholarship.

---

* The distance from the hash mark to the sideline in pro football is 70 feet 9 inches. I'm thrilled that you got it right.

15

The Day Fran and Jerry
Preempted the West Coast Offense

In the 1980s and '90s pro football lifted itself into what it is today—a socially acceptable flight from normalcy for tens of millions of Americans. It was propelled there by television, the competition of billionaire owners, the even more competitive drive of the athletes— and in no small part by an intriguing scheme of attack called the West Coast offense.

There's an irony there. At a time when so much of pro football's popularity grew with the New Age culture in entertainment on TV, this flashy new offense basically mobilized skills that most kids bring to the playground instinctively.

It was popularly identified with the San Francisco 49ers and Bill Walsh, the 49er coach, who made use of it to bring home a succession of Super Bowl rings during the 1980s. It's still functioning in a half dozen variations and relatively high visibility around the NFL today. Genius resists stagnation. In fact, at this very moment there are probably brilliant minds scheming new wrinkles in it. When it was at full momentum, in the hands of coaches like Walsh, Mike Holmgren, Mike Shanahan and Andy Reid, and such practitioners as Joe Montana, Jerry Rice, Brett Favre, and John Elway, it sent pro football in a new direction—spreading the field, shifting options on the fly, creating weaknesses in the defense and exploiting them.

To be effective, it required quarterbacks who could think on the run, receivers who could turn runners and runners who could catch. And while it was doing all that, it kept the other offense off the field.

Jerry Burns has some words of advice for Joey Browner

Its mantra: control the ball and you'll win the game.

Montana and Rice were among the first of the household heroes of the pro game to bring the new offense to the widening television audience—particularly the Super Bowl audience, which was beginning to swell to numbers unprecedented for sports attractions on television. One of the first dramatic moments of that Super Bowl era was the length-of-the-field drive that Montana, the unflappable Joe, conducted against the Cincinnati Bengals in the final seconds of the 1982 game. That drive almost equaled the extraordinary leaping catch made by Dwight Clark in the end zone to win the NFC championship for the 49ers against Dallas a few weeks earlier. It came on the last stroke of the clock—a play now imbedded in legend simply as the "The Catch."

The origins of the West Coast offense trace to the nimble mind of Sid Gillman, one of the coaching innovators of the 20th century; and to Walsh, who flourished after leaving the Cleveland Browns as a coaching assistant, resurrecting the football program at Stanford and then building a dynasty with three Super Bowl titles with the 49ers.

Their idea was to move downfield and control the clock with

quick, short passes, capitalizing on the ingenuity and versatility of both the quarterback and the receivers, and employing running backs as an essential part of the passing game. With the short game established, the deep passing game became a much higher percentage call. This was mixed with a running game that acquired added potency when one of the running backs was an accomplished pass receiver. Dominating possession of the ball was the ultimate goal and with that, of course, came scoring. Walsh set a goal of 25 first downs a game. Eventually he and others who used the system began scripting the first 10 or 15 plays ahead of time as a means of striking quickly from one play to the next, giving the defense minimal time to adjust and make substitutions. The system led to the no-huddle offense and other refinements we see in the game today.

But one night in Dallas in 1978, before the West Coast offense achieved the cult status it acquired in the 1980s, Jerry Burns and Francis Tarkenton of the Minnesota Vikings, choreographed a prologue that may very well have sped the arrival of Bill Walsh's revolution that followed.

Burns was leprechaun of a coach, an assistant to Grant as the Viking offensive coordinator. He later became the Viking head coach and just missed reaching the Super Bowl when a goal line pass squirted out of the hands of a receiver in the National Football Conference title game in Washington.

Burns was a grumbler and a virtuoso in the selective use of traditional four-letter words, which he sprinkled into his coaching conversation in place of duller but more conventional rhetoric. Yet he was a delight to his players and friends as a basically lovable guy, generous and affable away from the ball yard.

He was the head coach at Iowa for several years before moving to the Green Bay Packers, where he coached the offense on Vince Lombardi's two Super Bowl champions. Burns and Grant were well acquainted before that during Grant's years with the Winnipeg team in the Canadian League, and Burns joined the Viking staff as the offensive coordinator in 1968, Grant's second year as the Viking coach and what became the Vikings' first year in the league playoffs.

Burns' ultimate alliance with Tarkenton in the 1970s helped to make the Vikings one of pro football's annual powers, almost habitually in the Super Bowl of that era. None of this, of course, would have been likely without the presence of people like Grant, Alan Page, Paul Krause, Carl Eller, Chuck Foreman, Ron Yary, Jim Marshall, Ed White, Mick Tinglehoff, Jeff Siemon, Bill Brown and more. But Tarkenton turned the switch.

He was an altogether remarkable football player, although not especially adored in the press boxes. It may be that he didn't have the physical presence or the style of the standard heroic quarterback. Physically he was tough when injured and mentally he was usually one or two beats ahead of the defense and most of his interrogators. It took them a few years to elevate him to the Hall of Fame but fundamentally he was a winner. He was talkative and revealing after the game, win or lose, and seldom carried a grudge whatever treatment he got on Monday mornings. In the media grillings after the game he was spontaneous and confident. Sometimes he was rash in his judgments and off-the-cuff vocabulary.

It got him into trouble once when he was steamed up after being booed in a home game. In the locker room later he came with some heavy verbal artillery. Most experienced and successful quarterbacks around the league, he said, didn't receive that kind of treatment. They weren't booed, he said, they were "revered," an unfortunate choice of language by a bright guy who probably should have paused to consider a more appropriate word. It invited a lot of juicy rebuttals from his critics. It recurred years later when a reporter in Atlanta asked him to comment on Brett Favre's newest designs on his football reincarnation as a Minnesota Viking. Favre's scheme to throw in with a longtime rival of his former Green Bay Packers was, Francis declared, "despicable."

It may have been a lot of things, but "despicable," seemed to land somewhere in outer space as a description of Favre's conduct, odd as it seemed at the time.

But Francis usually spoke his mind and wasn't terrified by the fallout. He spent most of his early years as a skittering quarterback, and had to explain later that he was running (a) for his life and (b) to keep the play alive in his early role as the leader of a vagabond expansion team, the Vikings. Later he won championships with his arm as well as his head, and as the coach who knew him best—Grant—will tell you, he also won with his nerve and acceptance of pain. What kind of arm? Before Dan Marino and Brett Favre replaced it, he held the league record with 342 touchdown passes playing for the Vikings, Giants and again the Vikings.

And there was the game in Dallas in 1978. The Vikings had gone to their Super Bowls by then and were struggling to make the playoffs. Their great linemen were aging, and Tarkenton was in this 18th and final year.

In practice that week, Burns pulled him aside. "Let's work something (freaking) different," he said. Why not, Tarkenton said. Burns laid it out in the offense's squad meetings. They were going to spread the field. They were going run the offense on the fly. This was, remember, 1978. It had to begin with Tarkenton, and the game was on a rare Thursday night, on national television from Dallas.

For half a season the team had been groping in the crannies and bins for something that would ignite its offense. On Tuesday before the Dallas game, Burns showed his multiple offense schemes to Tarkenton and asked him what he thought. In pro football, the salesmanship starts with a coach. If the offensive coach can't sell the quarterback, especially one who's been there for eighteen years, they'll have to go back to leather helmets and the flying wedge. Tarkenton looked at the blueprints, slapped Burns on the head and said, "Burnsie I love it."

Burns is waspish little guy with no pretensions about making history. "Walsh and Gillman had been working in these things and God knows who else," he said later, "but most of the teams in that era where using standard pro sets with variations and the defenses were ready for them. Our season wasn't going very well up to that game so we thought, what the hell, let's try something else. Nobody was any better than Tarkenton thinking on the run. He gave us options any time he had the ball and no matter where he had it.

"And Foreman was one of the best receivers of all the league's running backs. We also had Bill Brown and Ricky Young as running backs, and both of them could catch and run. So some plays we'd put Foreman out there wide. Then we'd pull him back and send Ahmad Rashad and Sammy White out there. Some times it was Rickey Young. Tarkenton read the field and Foreman was a big threat no matter where he lined up. So we got the tight ends and the wide receivers involved, and once those things were on the plate, the running game really rolled."

Tarkenton reveled in it.

On that night, the line of scrimmage was his keyboard. The game turned into a recital, and the veteran quarterback, playing in his final season and probably knowing it, poured his personality and craft into it for three hours. He was nimble, smart, and cheeky, sometimes passionate and gung-ho. But the next play he would be the mechanic, adjusting and tinkering. Or he was downright brassy. He preferred to call it arrogant, because that's how he styled himself as a quarterback and it may have been one more reason he became a target for the critics.

To the Dallas Cowboys, Francis Tarkenton was something else. He was one stride, one idea and one stroke ahead of them all night. So to the rest of the Tarkenton resume that night, you could add maddening and, at the end, unbeatable.

At no time in his 18 years of pro football had Tarkenton been more empathically and euphorically the leader of his team. The game, in fact, might have summarized the peculiar mix of brains and gall that Tarkenton brought to football. There was his manipulation of the Vikings' hastily engineered ten-formation offense, one that plowed the programmed movement of the Dallas defense into disarray after ten minutes. But before he did that, he put on another hat in the Tarkenton collection. He was a soap peddler. For two days before the game he partnered with the gnarled little Burnsie. They were salesmen in the locker room, persuading their football team that these wild spread formations could work against a team that the previous year had been the best in football.

They conspired. It got to be a contagion. "I never was part of

179

anything like that in my life," one of the younger linemen, Frank Myers, said after the Vikings' 21-10 victory. "I never thought you could play a big game like that in the pros, people all over the field. The Cowboys are good, but it was like an ambush."

It was the essence of Tarkenton. It wasn't only the football Tarkenton. It was the Tarkenton with his chutzpah and his swash-buckling and his goads to make it work. With a guy like this, winning and being rich were only part of the allure. Making a joyride out of it was the other.

He came into pro football as a preacher's kid from Georgia, zesty and confident, but also with a likeable streak of the Sunday School disciple in him. When he left it to become a corporate man, he was still zesty and confident, also functionally hard-boiled, and probably with a few less beatitudes than when he started.

The Dallas defense that night came with its usual computerized sets, ready for the Tarkenton rollouts and for backs coming out at all angles as receivers. They were also going to keep Chuck Foreman under surveillance, and they were wary of Burns' gadgetry.

But what was this?

Foreman and Rickey Young shifted in and out of the I formation. Backs and receivers were spread to the sidelines. On one play they were looking at Ahmad Rashad and Sammy White abreast on the right flank. On the next play Rashad was practically in the backfield and White was almost out of sight. The Cowboys were in chaos and ultimately in jail.

And the man who carried the keys was Tarkenton. He threw while sprinting and backtracking. He threw on sudden counts and quick rhythms. When they tried to engulf him with blitzers, he threw blindly because his quick read of the Dallas defense told him nobody would be patrolling the field where he threw. And if the ball flew with anything resembling a spiral, Rashad, Young, White, or Foreman would eventually overtake it. When Dallas ganged his receivers and invited the run, Tarkenton sent Foreman pounding into the Dallas secondary.

No quality quarterback ever lived who didn't want the ball in his hands when the critical play came, Grant used to say. "You talk to them on the sideline. You ask them what's good on the goal line. Tarkenton was one of those guys who said, 'how about a rollout?' He meant he was going to find somebody open. He'd have time moving with the ball. Or he could run. And he'd promise you that if nothing was there, he'd throw it away. Other guys might say, 'Well, a draw play might work there.' That's the guy you don't want quarterbacking the team."

So during the week of the Dallas game, Tarkenton lobbied his team relentlessly. Nobody did huckstering in the locker room the way Tarkenton did. "It's not gimmicky," he said. "It's sound. The idea is to slow them down on their safety blitzes and the other blitzes. We have to spread them out and make them move and guess before we throw."

The pros, with all their hoary codes about what works, insist that it isn't formations that win games, it's players.

Sometimes formations help, especially when the players are Tarkenton, Rashad, Foreman, and those all-pro grunts on the offensive line.

Grant and Burns intended to hold off the new formations for three or four minutes to add the surprise element. But with the Vikings 28 yards from the Dallas goal line in the opening minutes, why temporize? Two minutes later they had the first touchdown, and a little later another. Dallas recovered in the second half but the Vikings won it, 21-10.

Nobody called it the birth of the West Coast Offense, Midwest Branch. It was a snapshot of what was coming. And someplace in front of a television set, Bill Walsh must have looked at it with a mixture of approval and annoyance. It was something he'd been preaching for years, and here it was on national television. A few years later Montana turned it into an institution.

16

Brad and Brett—

An Odd Pair on a Treasure Hunt

The coach of the Minnesota Vikings, Brad Childress, majored in psychology in college. Part of it was a serious study of abnormal behavior. He needed all of that to survive his first two years as the Viking coach, when his combined scorecard read 14 wins, 18 losses, while he groped around in search of a quarterback.

Unsettled as those two years were, they turned out to be a refuge of calm compared with the day Brett Favre began hearing voices again in the spring of 2009 while languishing in his second miserable retirement after 16 years of adulation with the Green Bay Packers.

What Favre was hearing again were the sounds of battle from distant scrimmage lines, where his psyche has always been tuned. He was at that stage in the waning career of a superhero where he was trying to orchestrate a grand finale, and life with the New York Jets in 2008 basically messed up the scenario. So he was now nearing 40, and looking.

None of this could have surprised or disappointed Childress, since one of Favre's first acts of unretirement after his divorce from the Packers was to try to find his way into the huddle of the Minnesota Vikings. So here was the coach, a division winner in 2008 but for all practical purposes still on probation and without a contract renewal in his fourth year. He had announced a competition between the career backup, Sage Rosenfels, and the struggling young Tarvaris Jackson, still on probation as an NFL quarterback.

Rosenfels and Jackson took it seriously. So, apparently, did

Childress. But the phonelines between the Vikings' Winter Park and Hattiesburg, Mississippi, informally open for more than a year, stayed open. Favre predictably announced a second retirement after the last month of the Jets' season went badly for him, in part because of his weakened throwing arm. A doctor was summoned, a procedure followed, Favre resumed his workouts with the high school receivers in Hattiesburg, and the circus was on.

All of the news and most of the rumors essentially originated from the big cable and internet sports desks in the east, where Favre and his agent had friends and de facto allies. This essentially froze out the colony of Twin Cities pro football writers, some of the better ones in the country. The requirements of the job put them in the dismal role of relaying the rumors to their audiences and having to identify the source.

Brad Childress

This is mentioned because of the outside chance that the Brett Favre scheme doesn't work out, and Brad Childress the psychology major—as the middleman and procurer of record—has to deal with some long memories. One of them is the suspicious Viking story line that Favre actually was serious about announcing his third and final retirement a few weeks after the medical procedure, but eagerly responded "yep" when Childress called with a final invitation. It was made, not coincidentally, at the end of the Vikings training camp in Mankato, a fact that most of the insiders assumed was part of a deal to accommodate Favre's organic distaste for training camps

Childress is genuinely a man of values, accountability being high on the list. Ultimately he is accountable for what happens with his team. But until the arrival of Brett Favre, it WAS Childress' team. For all practical purposes in 2009, it's Favre's team in the minds of most of the fans, never mind that the Vikings under Childress and with Adrian Peterson won 10 games and the division title last year with mediocrity at quarterback. It becomes the coach's team again in 2009 if it loses more than expected. Childress the psychologist knows that and isn't going to argue with it. Favre was available. If he wins, the Vikings win, Childress wins and the fans are in heaven. Before Favre reported, the Wilf management had already endorsed a contract maximizing at $25 million for two years, with major subtractions if he plays only one year or less.

The scene when he arrived at the Vikings' Winter Park in Eden Prairie outperformed all previous ecstasies bestowed on presidents and show biz immortals arriving in Minnesota. Helicopters whirled overhead. Vastly outnumbered cops grappled gamely but futilely with the crowds. The motorcade arrived from the airport and Favre jerseys blotted out the sun. At times it resembled the triumphant march from *Aida*. This was a 39-year-old football player who holds all the records, returning to his lifelong sandbox, the football field, and the frenzy of the fans was off the charts. But around the country the blogosphere was filled with a fury of insults traded by Packer and Viking zealots. Some of the stars of the national media were offended less by the scene than by the decision—not so much Favre's as the Vikings.

In San Francisco, Gwen Knapp of the *Chronicle* railed, "Favre's flip-flopping could taint him forever…Favre's fickle approach to retirement is an embarrassment that should follow him forever. For a quarterback, indecisiveness reflects incapacity. An indecisiveness that keeps you out of training camp reflects a supreme failure of leadership…"

To his considerable audience, *Sports Illustrated*'s Peter King preached: "Childress has looked like a desperate man throughout this melodrama. He made it known internally that Favre had to do at least some work in the offseason program or the veteran mini-camp to be considered. Favre never showed. Then he had to come by the start of camp. Favre didn't come, opting for his third false retirement in 17 months. Now the Vikings let him come back after the team has gone through training camp. Favre's the wishy-washiest player in memory—and the Vikings are his enablers. It's ridiculous."

But nearing 40, Favre is convinced he is still strong enough and competitive enough to play with a winner; not only to play for it but to lead it. To Favre it means that he still belongs as a frontline star. These are the sentiments of an old warrior trying to regain the cachet of his professional life. You think of Favre and you remember the quote from the World War II general, George S. Patton, the crusty Blood and Guts George. He would talk philosophically about battle and clash of arms. "God forgive," he would say, "I love it so."

Brett Favre in calmer times

Playing quarterback isn't leading a division of tanks. But playing quarterback is what Favre does. He quit once after the 2007 season partly because he couldn't handle the despair of throwing a game-killing interception when the Packers might have made it to the Super Bowl. It's one memory he wants to redeem.

And his partner now becomes Brad Childress. Aside from his academic background in psychology, Childress, being a pro football coach, had to arm himself with some basic defenses for the sometimes fragile human psyche when it's hammered by random shocks. For coaches, missing the playoffs is one. Blowing a two touchdown lead in the fourth quarter is another. They are a routine part of the landscape in professional football. So consider Brad Childress approaching the 2009 season which, especially with Favre, is the critical one. His team in 2008 won ten games, a divisional title and made the playoffs. Winning ten games and making the playoffs is now the standard. Winning ten games in 2009 is acceptable. Missing the playoff is not.

This is not a dimwit exercise in numerology. This is the National Football League. Ten coaches in the NFL lost their jobs during or after the 2008 season. It was about average.

Childress became the Viking head coach in 2006 after a successful tour as the offensive coordinator of the Philadelphia Eagles that included an appearance in the Super Bowl and a significant role in the development of quarterback Donovan McNabb.

The falling bricks started before he got to Minnesota. During the season prior to Childress's arrival in Minnesota, a platoon of Viking players chartered a cruise boat on Lake Minnetonka, invited some companionable women on board and turned the day into what became known as the Loveboat Scandal of 2005. It ignited a legal soap opera that stretched for months into 2006 and plagued Childress's first season with the Vikings.

Also during the previous season, Daunte Culpepper, the veteran Pro Bowl quarterback who would have been the centerpiece of Childress's offense, suffered a severe knee injury that might have mended with good professional therapy. On the brink of Childress's first season, Culpepper decided he could supervise his physical rehabilitation in Florida better than the Vikings' trained staff could do it in Minnesota. This precipitated an impasse with the Vikings, who eventually traded him to Miami, leaving Childress's new team with a fading Brad Johnson at quarterback.

A few weeks before the start of the season, Koren Robinson, who had the potential to become a star receiver, was arrested after being clocked at 104 miles an hour in a 55 mph zone near the Viking training camp in St. Peter, MN. He was charged with DWI and fleeing police, his second alcohol-related arrest as a pro football player. Robinson didn't catch a huge amount of passes for the Vikings in 2006. Neither did anyone else.

And for historians it couldn't be forgotten that a year before Childress took the job in Minnesota, the Vikings traded away their one world-class asset, the pass-catching wonderchild, Randy Moss, who had grown weary of his exertions in Minnesota.

Childress's predictable 6-10 first season as the Vikings' coach offered very little to love. He was a puzzle to most of the professional critics and many of the players. Add most of the fans, who hadn't especially approved of the rough-housing Mike Tice or the slightly paranoid (if successful) Denny Green, but at least understood them.

Childress gave the appearance of a man of precision and organization. These are not normally terms of disapproval but they lose their luster when the coach in question is racking up losses. He was organized. He spoke fluently and with assurance, and presented a kind of mustached dapperness you might have expected from an agent of M5 handing James Bond his survival kit. He was clearly a man committed to values and principles, as a coach and private citizen. But in football those attributes are usually admired more enthusiastically when Ws follow on the scoreboard.

Although critics and fans alike had been hard on both Tice and Green, Childress's honeymoon was short, and the scrutiny being focused on his coaching style since then has never been lathered with kindness. His early sideline image—holding his play card under his trim mustache to protect his calls from prying lip-readers in the stadium booths—became a caricature among his critics.

Earlier in his career, when Childress coached quarterbacks or managed the offense, much of the heat fell on the head coach or the quarterbacks. But during his first two seasons in Minnesota the Vikings went 6-10 and 8-8 and failed to make the playoffs. Now he was in the crosshairs. So how does a football coach like Brad Childress deal with the sharpshooting?

"It got easier," he said, "when I realized these folks (the writers, especially, and broadcasters) have a role to play."

That role? Critic. Giver of Wisdom. Sometimes the wise guy who needs a foil. It's part of the work environment for anybody who puts his or her handicraft before the public today. In earlier days the roasting of a troubled coach was relatively sedate. Today it's a feeding frenzy. It's sometimes unfair or premature or downright cheap. Unless the performer understands it or learns how to deal with it, the pressure can eat him up.

It also got easier for Childress when he began looking at what provoked some of the sniping. He was often pictured as a stiff, nerdy kind of guy, a serious reader capable of describing the atmosphere in the Vikings run-up to the playoffs as "the urgency of now." It was a crisp literary allusion, in fact a good one. But it sounded vaguely like Tony Blair in the House of Commons rather than an NFL coach in the 14th game of the season. He was whimsically being invited by some in the Viking press corps to loosen up.

And so he has. It took him a while to get comfortable with the rules of the road in his relationships with the media, but it was relief all around when he decided there are times when he enjoys the gamesmanship and plays it well.

Last winter an exchange took place between Childress and Bob Sansevere of the *St. Paul Pioneer Press* after the Vikings won their 10th game of the season by beating the defending NFL Super Bowl champions, the New York Giants.

S. "You have more of a sense of humor than a lot of people realize. Why don't you show it more often?"

C. "You're not up there to be a comedian."

S. "You just won the division. If you're going to be funny, now is the time."

C. "I'm not a five-minutes-on-Johnny Carson guy. I enjoy a good laugh as much as anybody, probably dry humor."

S. "I noticed after Sunday's game and also last week that you seemed to be testy about the criticism you've been receiving. Is winning the division an 'in your face' to your critics?"

C. "I don't think you want to gloat. I think [when I talked with an edge] it was because, usually, I saw my predecessor's [Mike Tice] record at 9-7, and I was told I couldn't get to 9-7. The Bears didn't play anybody in that final game. They didn't play their starting quarterback at all and about three or four of the starters."

S. "So it was the criticism that ([Mike Tice) got to 9-7 and you hadn't gotten there that bothered you."

C. "Yeah. I know this. I don't care how you get to double-digit wins. I think there are 10 teams this year with double-digit wins, and it's hard. It's very hard."

S. "Do you feel vindicated?"

C. "I'm not looking for vindication. I'm just a career football coach who believes I have a good vision and a good plan for this organization, and I've got a good bunch of guys."

S. "You're one of the few coaches I know who doesn't mind letting people see your bald head. If you have a big playoff run, do you think you can make bald 'chic?' Maybe you should start thinking about it. If you keep winning, guys may start shaving their head to look like you."

C. "I had [a coach] ask me one time, 'Hey, Chill, you and I ought to get a weave. What do you think about getting a weave?' I said, 'A what?' He goes, 'A weave. They've got these great weave things.' I said, 'first, you have to have something to weave. And B, I'm not interested. If (the hair) goes, it goes."

S. "The fans at the last game were given an Adrian Peterson mask on a stick...Do you think there might be a Brad Childress mask?"

C. "Jared Allen is trying to talk my wife into having me grow a

189

mullet. I saw him at dinner the other night. He said, 'She's in for it. She's thinking that's the way to go. Only real men wear mullets.' I said, "What am I going to do with the top?"

S. "You can do the comb-over."

It was easy banter with the press—easier, of course, when you win. But it might actually come closer to the core Brad Childress, probably one of the more interesting guys you're going to meet in the business, once he has the traction to reveal more of himself—which, of course, comes with winning.

The acceptance started to come, not coincidentally, about the time his team won those ten games and with the growing evidence that Childress, working with the Viking personnel people and scouting system, had by the fall of 2009 assembled a team capable of going deep into the playoffs, perhaps as a significant Super Bowl contender.

Something needs to be remembered about making it in the big time atmospherics of today. For the coaching lifer, the Shangri La in today's football is the day a media conference is called hurriedly, probably to beat ESPN, and a smiling man in a Brooks Brothers suit introduces the next head coach in the National Football League.

Under today's salary schedules in the NFL, that's the day when he becomes a certified millionaire; within reach are added millions that the successful coaches are drawing today, a few close to $8 million a year.

It's more than the money, of course. The job of head coaching in the NFL is the ultimate validation of years of struggle in the ranks, thousands of hours of squinting at film and tape, barking and hustling in the workouts, scheming something new, tense interviews, climbing the ladder, making an impression, infighting for some, unemployment when the guard changes, worries about the family.

Most, but not all, of the good ones in coaching advance. For Childress and for most of the coaches, the struggle for survival renews each year. And why is 2009 a year when Childress may need to dredge up all of the specialized knowledge of the human behavior that he learned in college?

The Vikings' 2008 season of 10 wins and 6 losses is usually considered a major achievement in the NFL. They made the playoffs but lost to Philadelphia in the first round. The team approached the 2009 season with the best defensive line in the league, an adequate offensive line, and the most spectacular running back in football, Adrian Peterson. And now Favre.

They got an earlier upgrade with the drafting on the first round of Percy Harvin of Florida, whose behavioral sheet didn't look as promising as his time in the 40-yard-dash, his pass-catching attributes and his potential as a wildcat runner. The question marks dropped him to 21st in the draft, where Childress and the Vikings joyously grabbed him. This may have been another Viking coup on the scale of Denny Green's steal of the quirky but supremely gifted Randy Moss a decade earlier. Time will make the only judgment there.

At the time, this relatively minor stir of aggressiveness in the player markets provoked little passion among the Viking masses. It offered no hint of the theatrics and the media sideshow ahead for the ultimate arrival of Favre.

But the acquisition of Sage Rosenfels provided one more snapshot of the trials of a football coach facing a critical season and a skeptical audience.

Rosenfels was brought in as a 31-year-old veteran, a big and bright guy with a strong arm and a workable dossier as a backup quarterback in a variety of NFL venues.

The stated objective was a competition between Rosenfels and the part-time incumbent, Tarvaris Jackson. Over the previous three years the Viking crowds revealed an overwhelming lack of enthusiasm for Brad Johnson, Brooks Bollinger and Kelly Holcomb, the stand-in quarterbacks for the developing Jackson, who had been a surprise—some people said inexplicable—second round draft choice by the Vikings in Childress's first year. Jackson played for a small college and was an unknown to the football audiences. Once launched, he had supporters; but he, too, was viewed suspiciously by most of the critics. His play was uneven. He was mobile and could throw but his decision-making was suspect. The reaction to Gus Frerotte, the original backup in the Childress scheme, was similarly mixed. He was a good old professional with a reliable arm but no mobility, and he was gone after the 2008 season.

Rather proudly, the Vikings announced the acquisition of Sage Rosenfels in late February hoping for a positive reaction from the critics to help juice up enthusiasm for the Vikings in the middle of an economic crunch. Simultaneously, Frerotte was released.

The reaction:

Wrote Tom Powers of the *St. Paul Pioneer Press*:

"Yippee, another mediocre quarterback. The Vikings are collecting them."

Wrote the *Star Tribune*'s Mark Craig: "An attempt was made to get excited on Day 1 of the Sage Rosenfels era. Sorry, I got nothin'."

Through most of his coaching career, Childress was shielded from that kind of heat—which, when you think about it, is low Fahrenheit compared with the blow-torch commentary that is broadly practiced today.

A week later, Matt Birk, one of the most respected Vikings and a veteran of the Pro Bowls, flew to Baltimore and signed a $12 million contract, with $6 million guaranteed, to play center for the Ravens, making no reference to the Vikings' obvious lack of interest in keeping him on the payroll.

So Brad Childress, what did all of this say for the chances of success in a pivotal season for the coach—and the team?

"There is pressure in this game, yes. It's pressure on everyone. How do you handle the pressure? Sometimes we can laugh about that, your job and mine, for example. Could you do a job if your livelihood depended on an oblong object that doesn't bounce regularly?"

Without a doubt, bad bounces are energetically to be avoided. In Childress's job they can't be. He learned some time ago that a coach's chances of limiting the bad bounces have something to do with the players' character. Skilled players, experience, and leadership may have something more to do with it. But very often the difference between a championship or less will reflect the atmosphere in the locker room and those elusive things called will and commitment, sacrifice and extra effort—and values. Most coaches will concur. But they will also agree that these things are often hard to quantify, although they are highly prized.

Childress has tried to measure it or, perhaps more accurately, to predict it. Some time ago at a squad meeting he put up a card, a kind of power point, listing the parts of his life that mattered to him. His first two entries were Faith and Family. He listed others. He asked the players to do the same.

"I asked them to be honest," he said. They weren't prejudicing themselves, he let them know, if their list included interests not on the dean's list of behavior or fun stuff. There were other needs, like money and respect. Most of the players took the list seriously. Some didn't. "I asked them not to put down things like family and telling the truth if you're a guy who likes to hang out at strip clubs and has extra-marital affairs. If you really believe in hard work and earning trust, then put them down."

The coach said he would read the cards. He said he wouldn't do it in a judgmental way, but he would periodically talk to the players: "How are you doing with these things that you put down, your hard work, your achievements?"

If any prior raps on Childress included a reluctance to take risks in his relations with players, that exercise pretty much erased them. Toward what end?

"It gives me a window with these players when they come into this office. It doesn't make any difference how they got here. I'd like to see values like the ones I admire. It's taken me 30 years to get into this place. I think I bring principles that guide me in bringing in good people, who know right from wrong. I think it has something to do with the fiber within you and how you acquired it. It's a fiber you want to see in your players.

"And so when the going gets tough I know what I'm going to get from that guy. Integrity is a great word. You can build a culture with that in the locker room. When you first come in, it's what you look for. It takes time. You see things you don't like. Three years ago there were dogs coming through this locker room, including Dobermans, and guys you never saw before walking through it. You'd ask somebody, 'Who's that, and what's he doing in this locker room?' There was dog crap in the place, and I had to say, 'Guys, this is your office. You can bring your young sons in here, but not the guy from your home town. This **is our place, the team's.'**

"One thing I remember about Bill Walsh, a great man and coach, and I share it with players. 'Don't be the guy who doesn't get it,' Bill Walsh would say. 'Don't be the guy, when we travel, who is standing there in a bookstore and buys a *Playboy* magazine and pulls it out and stands there looking at the centerfold and there's a 4-year-kid looking at him. Don't be that guy.'

"Don't be the guy," Childress will add, "who walks out of this building and gets a DUI on Hwy 494. I can't be impressed about a guy's athleticism on tape if I'm worried that he's going to rob a store on his way home.

"So I've tried to be as direct as I could be with guys who should know where they stand. You add and subtract, building a team. And I think we have a good team. We won 10 games in 2008, and some big games to get into the playoffs."

I told the story about George Allen telephoning from the cot in his office at 3 a.m. on a Saturday before a big playoff game with the Vikings.

Childress smiled with some irony. "I can't top that, but I did over-night in the office when I was in Philadelphia. That (cot-in-the-office) takes its toll. I did it here with the Vikings in my first year. Then I said, 'Wait a minute.' You need to take time off to go home and sleep in your bed. I missed a ton of things that are important to the kids when I was not being an 8 to 5 dad. You miss those times when one of your children would come and sit next to you, and get the feet back and you'd just sit there together.

"One thing I can tell you for sure. When you live that kind of life, one thing you need is a tremendously strong wife."

Whatever his fate in 2009, Childress is not likely to be backing down on his conviction that putting enough "good guys" together makes a winner. If he began as a mystery to the fans, it wasn't that much different with the players. He seemed to many of them to be giving lectures. First impressions by the players may not kill you but they can load you down.

In his second season Childress and the Vikings withheld receiver Troy Williamson's weekly check of $25,500 for leaving the team for nine days and missing its Nov. 4 game with San Diego after the death of his maternal grandmother. Williamson was a first round draft choice of the Vikings but rarely performed well and was generally a dartboard for the team's critics. Most teams in the NFL do not allow players extended time beyond the customary few days when there is a death in the family. The Vikings declined to pay Williamson for the week he missed, deeming the nine days excessive. Childress called it a "business principle," perhaps not the best use of the English language.

Williamson objected and found sympathy from many of his teammates. The matter came up at the weekly meeting between Childress and some of the more respected team veterans who form a players' council. Childress invites them to speak freely and candidly when they meet with him.

The players supported Williamson's case. Childress told the *Star Tribune* afterward: "They were thoughtful, productive and positive. We spoke at length about [the Williamson matter]. The intent of the leadership group is to have productive discussion and to serve as a conduit for the rest of the team. The big thing we talked about is that everyone grieves differently."

Childress also discussed the issue with the Viking ownership. The Vikings reversed themselves and made full payment to Williamson, who then announced that the money would be given to a charitable foundation.

Here was a case of a clear-cut violation of what seemed to be a sensible rule. But a substantial number of the team's veterans supported the player, who was a problematic one. Childress and the ownership could have insisted on upholding the rule. At what cost?

Two weeks later, the Vikings began a five-game winning streak that nearly lifted them into the playoffs.

A coincidence?

Probably not. The next year they reached the playoffs. Growth, to players and coach, comes in a variety of ways, and sometimes at unpredictable times.

If the team lands in the playoffs, you can credit growth. If it doesn't, nobody talks much about growth or character cards. When you sign on to coach in the NFL, you do it with extra money in the bank but with no illusions.

So with their one stab at bringing in a high-asset player in the 2009 player draft in April, the Vikings and Childress chose the multi-talented Percy Harvin, who had tested positive for marijuana during the player combine preview to the draft.

His resume also posted other questionable behavior. Childress made a point of visiting with the player and family before the draft. They emerged all smiles at the first news conference in Minneapolis after the draft and Childress received a virtually unanimous 4.0 from the media critics in the early reviews.

Coaches, even the highly principled ones, sometimes make decisions that seem logical enough when you throw survival into the mix.

It's a dilemma well understood in the National Football League.

17

Whither Wilf and the Vikings in 2010?

The Minnesota Vikings were granted a franchise in the National Football League in 1960 with a down payment of $600,000.

That's $600,000, with only five zeroes. When the rest of the entry fee was delivered later in the year the total payment came to $1 million, for membership in what is now the richest conglomerate in American sports, the NFL.

The most recent numbers put the value of the Viking franchise at somewhere close to $800 million, which would make it 32nd and last in the NFL in franchise value, according to Forbes Magazine.

The reason for the Vikings tail-end status in those computations is the relatively humble revenue stream flowing out of the Humphrey Metrodome, where the team has played since 1982. The Viking income from their add-on club suites is outweighed by the millions flowing into the vaults of teams playing in newer stadiums that offer fancier aeries for their priority guests and customers.

When the Vikings finish the 2009 season the larger struggle will begin to determine if the team is going to stay in Minnesota. Its stadium lease runs out in 2011. What happens next year may be traumatic for everybody involved, including the fans, team, ownership—and the taxpayers. The big and mind-stretching new chip may be Brett Favre.

The Viking ownership is headed by Zygi Wilf, an amiable real estate developer from the East Coast, who with other family members bought the team for $600 million in 2005. The Wilfs brought with them zero experience in the management of a professional football team. They did bring reasonable calm and common sense and order to an organization that had slipped into a runamuck parody of management and was looking for buyers. The Wilfs came with big bucks and gradually changed the culture, although the team didn't hit stride on the field until last year. In the meantime the new owners showed no bashfulness in spending money to improve the team, which after four years of their stewardship won ten games in 2008 and reached the playoffs for the first time in the Wilf administration.

But the libretto of the approaching political grand opera involving the Wilfs, the Minnesota political structure and the tax-paying public is roughly this:

Everybody connected with it wants to keep the Vikings in Minnesota, including Zygi Wilf. His willingness to gamble by bringing in Favre for large millions is clear enough. What's bothering some of the citizens is his stadium numbers. The Vikings say that they can afford to stay if the Minnesota public, through its elected lawmakers, is willing to pay roughly three fourths of the projected stadium cost of some $950 million, which undoubtedly will climb in the reality.

A lot of tax-payers find that prescription pill hard to swallow. It's even harder for legislators who would have to sign off on it, and then explain to the voters why nearly three-quarters of a billion dollars for a retractable-roof stadium is more important than the education and public assistance programs that were trimmed or eliminated in the midst of the 2009 depression. With the nation in an economic nose-dive that has thrown millions out of work and/or out of their houses, provoked a virtual collapse of the banking system and forced major industries into bankruptcy, the auspices couldn't be much worse for building a new palace in which millionaire players cavort in front of other millionaires in their elite executive suites.

In the midst of this ongoing crisis, public enthusiasm for underwriting an athletic arena for wealthy football entrepreneurs is not sizzling on the front burner.

"We understand this," Zygi Wilf said. "Pro football is also being the Vikings are on television between 60 and 70 percent of the TV sets in Minnesota are tuned to our game. That's better than anywhere in the country (in terms of state or regional interest in an NFL team)."

Will that translate into popular support for a scheme in which the taxpayers are nicked for $700 million dollars to fund a stadium?

Zygi Wilf

It is not going to be an easy sell, in the Minnesota Legislature or in the cities and cornfields. But if the state does not come up with a substantial portion of the funds needed to build a new stadium, there is a very real possibility that the Vikings could invoke a nuclear option, leave the state and end 50 years of major league pro football in Minnesota. A second and less likely option for the Wilfs would be to sell the team.

Wilf declines to make those threats personally. He said at the end of the 2008 season that he had not been involved in any talks with the promoter of a new, privately-built stadium in Los Angeles, which if it materializes, will certainly attract a pro football team back to Los Angeles. It's a prospect made to order for Viking lobbyists. Wilf doesn't want to make a pitch based on threats. "All I want to say about that is that I'm disappointed we haven't gotten further than we have with our stadium proposal."

Which does not mean that everybody in the Viking organization is muzzled about the possibility of the team heading west.

Four and five years ago, the Minnesota Twins, the University of Minnesota and the Vikings all lobbied independently, and sometimes simultaneously, for new stadiums hinged to public cash. It got to be

199

Minnesota and the Vikings all lobbied independently, and sometimes simultaneously, for new stadiums hinged to public cash. It got to be a stadium du jour. The Vikings and Anoka County north of the Twin Cities were engaged for nearly two years in negotiations that ultimately pancaked. Part of the reason was Wilf's belief that downtown Minneapolis was going to be more fruitful in the long run. Accordingly, he purchased property near the Metrodome with a view to developing it as part of a broader investment involving a new stadium. As a business strategy it made sense, although it did stiffen the predictable resistance to a taxpayer subsidy for a new stadium.

Wilf is not a hotwired, belligerent guy. His speech is informal and unprovocative. The edgier argument for public support of a new stadium usually comes from the team's vice president of public affairs and stadium point man, Lester Bagley, who publicly invited the Minnesota governor, Tim Pawlenty, to exercise livelier leadership on the issue.

Bagley is a longtime professional in public affairs, stadium issues and lobbying. He hears almost every day the taxpayer argument about hitting the Vikings with a bigger share of the stadium costs, and told the website Sports Headliners:

"That argument was made to the Twins. The average private contribution, including in this market with the Twins, has been about 30 percent. Hennepin County put in about 70 percent (of the new Twins' stadium costs). They (the costs) have grown on the private side as the Twins have made some independent decisions to upgrade. The average through the NFL is about one-third private (meaning contributions by the club) particularly in this size market. The Wilfs' contribution stands up well both locally and nationally. The other side of it is it's a publicly-owned facility used by the public year around for amateur, high school, and college sporting events and tournaments. There's a community benefit there."

Wilf took the position that the Vikings' turn would come after the Target Stadium of the Twins and the TCF Bank Stadium for the University of Minnesota football team cleared the political hurdles. They did. The university's new stadium opens this fall, the Twins' in work it out with the public. Now we think it's our time. I think there is an idea that the taxpayers are just being asked to make rich owners richer. That's just not what this is. We need public support to build the stadium. They needed a new stadium in Indianapolis, which is a market comparable to ours, and the state paid all of it. We're not asking that. We're not going to get richer. We lose revenue sharing we get from the NFL when the stadium is built. There are other expenses..."

Such as the $15 million or so that it would cost the Vikings to play in the university stadium while theirs was being constructed on the site of the demolished Metrodome.

But, Wilf was asked, if the Vikings can't afford more than the $250 million, shouldn't they solicit help from their corporate neighbors in Minneapolis, who are presumably civic minded in the grand tradition and would stand to gain financially from a new stadium?

They might have years ago. But the times are pretty much past when promoters could go to family business titans such as the Pillsburys or the Daytons. Or to friendly banks. Or to the Minneapolis Star Tribune and the Cowles family, which might have been the single most important force in the passage and the construction of the Metrodome.

Why can't they do that now?

Well, which bank? The old Northwestern bank is now run out of California and is called Wells Fargo. What about Twin City Federal, which was in the thick of sponsorship of Minnesota Gopher football, and more?

Twin City Federal, TCF Bank, is now the name of the new university football stadium and it paid millions for the rights. Dayton's is now Macys. Target, the creation of Dayton's, paid for the naming rights to the Twins new stadium.

So where could the Vikings go for naming rights?

How about Minnesota Taxpayers Stadium?

It would be an original. It would also meet the test of reality. It would, in effect, be the taxpayers' stadium, or public stadium, in the hands of the stadium commission. It would probably provide enough high revenue suites to keep the Vikings in pursuit of their first Super Bowl championship. It would probably attract, as part of a quid pro quo arranged by the National Football League, a Super Bowl championship game sometime relatively soon after the grand opening.

However heated the forthcoming clashes, there is one ultimate test of the wisdom or justification of forcing the taxpayers to underwrite a capital improvement whose income primarily benefits private business.

The test is a simple one: "Is it in the public interest."

In a book written several years after the construction of the Metrodome, the now-Senator Amy Klobuchar asked that question in connection with the interplay of public and private interests in the evolution of the Metrodome. The book raised two questions: Did the process meet that test—years of hearings on the question, from border to border and in the legislature. The answer was yes. There were no angles that were not explored in the almost endless round of hearings, no questions that were not raised.

Then, did the actual result of those negotiations—the performance of the Metrodome—meet that test. The answer again was "yes." Major league baseball stayed in Minnesota. Ultimately the Twins won two World Series, drew reasonably well most of the time and remarkably well some of the time. The Vikings played to sell-outs every Sunday. The stadium made a profit for the public into the millions, enough for the Vikings and the Twins to absorb the endless drumbeat of ridicule—over the Teflon sky, baseballs disappearing in space, and—in Mike Ditka's unforgettable rant—"this is football in a cow barn."

It may be that, still. Yet the availability of that stadium for other events that are very much part of the community is another test of its value—what Lester Bagley might call "a recreation room" for the public.

But the Metrodome was built with bonds, and the taxpayers were never seriously nicked. However, funding a new football stadium, with a retractable roof, worth a billion dollars is, in the political clash it will evoke, like turning on the floodlights after the penny candles.

Here that ultimate test introduces one more element in the algebra of "is it in the public interest?"

The most significant community interest of all may be one to which the dollar sign cannot be attached. How important is it, in the broader community of 5 million people in the state of Minnesota, to have a professional football team in a league with the stature of the National Football League? That is, how real is the public identification with a football team?

That answer is going to swing wildly with the success or flops of that team. But there is no question that there have been seasons when the baseball or football teams, and other teams in other arenas, have created moments or days of public euphoria and pride, of hundreds of thousands of people coming together as an identifiable community. And those communities endure year after year, for all of the sneers when the team is lousy and the railing when the team goes into a funk. Although memories fade, such communities never quite desert the team. So the public does have a stake in a stadium and can be asked to make a contribution. The serious question is in the fairness of the figure.

In 2010 a juggling act will begin in earnest among the politicians, the fans, the ownership and the taxpayers. It will run for months. It can't run forever. The NFL will raise some warning flags, the Los Angeles piece will get bigger, and the state of Minnesota will ultimately have to make a decision in the midst of the rising political storm warnings.

Estimates that construction would provide 13,500 new jobs may or may not be accurate. They are part of the pressure. The stadium promoters also predict that over half of the total cost will take the form of wages and salaries. Who knows? Unions and corporate leaders are enlisted in the battle. Advocates for economic and social justice will yell.

But will the early $250 million offering of the Vikings on a billion dollar price tag be enough to meet a companion test: In fairness to the community, is the $700 million it is be asked to pay too much?

In the context of a continuing financial turmoil in America, it is. In almost any context, it's excessive.

Have the Vikings left themselves some wiggle room? One would hope so.

Would the loss of a professional football destroy the community? Not likely.

It would make it duller. It would dissolve that hand-slapping wackiness that rolls through the stadium and the town and in front of a million TV sets when our guys win a big one or Theee Big One.

Is that part of the equation?

It is. A bigger part is being right with all of these people in splitting the cost. That present split, the public's $700 million against the chief beneficiary's $250 million, isn't exactly right.

You always have to pause when you're linking the Minnesota public with the rest of the sporting publics around the country. Minnesotans tend to express their euphoria a little differently. The Twins won the World Series for the second time in 1991. It was Sunday night, a sensational pitching performance by Jack Morris at the Metrodome, and the Twins defeated Atlanta in seven games. The stadium fans, of course, celebrated in the stadium, the players mingled with them, and when it came time to head outdoors into the night, the crowds were suitably jubilant. But no light poles capsized and no cars were overturned. No riot squads were summoned.

There was one police call in suburban St. Louis Park. One of the Twins fans got out of hand and drove through the streets, beeping his horn in triumph at 1 a.m.

He was pulled over on a citizen complaint and charged with disturbing the peace.

So Zygi Wilf and his brother Mark Wilf will find themselves in the middle of the action in 2010. How well the Vikings do in 2009 will influence the negotiations, no doubt; more will be heard about and from Los Angeles. The NFL itself will come in with some experienced arm twisters and earnest-talking persuaders who will reveal how pained the NFL and America would be to see Minnesota lose the Vikings.

how pained the NFL and America would be to see Minnesota lose the Vikings.

And the process will play out. You would characterize Zygi Wilf as the kind of owner you'd like to see hang around. He entered the pro football business from the East Coast as a fan, a longtime admirer of the New York Giants. He clearly knows business. But pro football is a different kind of business and he leaves it primarily to a staff of people who know it better. Chiefly these are Bob Brzezinski, who runs football operations, negotiates the contracts and supervises the salary cap, and Rick Spielman, who oversees the scouting, drafting and trades. Both work closely with the coach in the strategic work of upgrading the player personnel and making deals that make sense.

Perhaps significantly, the Vikings do not have a de facto general manager running the full show. Wilf himself would meet that definition on the business side. Football operations no, and he acknowledges that. He bought the team after the rarely-a-dull-moment tenure of Red McCombs, who ran the franchise like an upscale used car operation, compulsively alert for a better deal—which turned out to be the one offered by Zygi Wilf and family.

"What we wanted was to find the right guys—players who would fit not only on the field but in the locker room," Wilf says. "We have moved in that direction. Getting into the playoffs is important. But what we want is to make steady progress toward those goals of building a team of players we think will fit in with that idea. We HAVE made progress. This is a very competitive league but there are teams— like Philadelphia, New England, Indianapolis, Pittsburgh—that are up there pretty high in most years. That's what we're aiming for here. I think the fans see that. If you don't have a great quarterback you can still be a winner. You can win with a shutdown defense, which we've done." And now, they have the icon, Brett Favre, at quarterback, thanks primarily to Wilf. The question is: Where is all of this going to be happening a couple of years from now?

We may know sooner than that.

18

When the Human Side
of Football Transcends
the Violence and Extravaganza

He had the craggy and weathered face of a man wandering home from the wars. His battlegrounds were the football fields across the country where he had coached, and he had the look of a tough and tested man who had seen it all.

But now the game was over and he couldn't stop his tears. He seemed momentarily lost in the jubilation on the Baltimore Ravens' sidelines, where players and coaches were crowding around his son, John Harbaugh, whose team had just beaten the Tennessee Titans in the biggest game of his coaching life.

For 10 or 15 seconds the camera came in close on the older man, and I remember wishing it could give us a few more, because every father watching the scene understood what was written on the face of this veteran football man. It was saying "All those years John put in as a coach...the hours of work, wins and disappointment." All of that was washed away.

The old man might have preferred to be alone, watching on TV, because there he could vent freely and maybe even talk. Here on the field he just wandered aimlessly for awhile. Jack Harbaugh the elder had coached at colleges across the country, a good coach but an itinerant coach. He remembered his younger son, Jim, now coaching at Stanford, being raked by the crowd when he quarterbacked the Bears.

But here was deliverance and pride. It was in Jack Harbaugh's tears and his willingness to wait until the proper moment to embrace his son. He was without words.

Without being a marshmallow about it, I think I have prized the human side of football even more than the tensions and the clash of driven and motivated athletes competing on the biggest stage of their sport.

I remember the day Walter Payton, the Bears' great running back, died after a long struggle with illness. He was only 47. No one who has ever played the game surpassed Walter Payton in the degree of respect and affection he stirred in every man who had played with him or against him. I wrote that day:

Pro football is big and boisterous and often brutal. It is also glamorous and rich and overblown and sometimes heroic. There are times when it is so big and visible it is simply engulfing and comes very close to the preposterous.

Pro football has earned all of those characterizations and more. One thing it is rarely called is beautiful. But for one brief and unforgettable moment, in the aftermath of the death of Walter Payton, it shed its bombastic image and became beautiful.

And why was that? The language doesn't seem to fit. The game is about spectacle and the clash of powerful and driven men colliding with other powerful and driven men. How are you going to extract beauty out of all that violence on the field, with the brassiness of the show business booming around it?

Yet in the hours following the death of Walter Payton, a solidarity of grief united the players, coaches and fans and seemed to dissolve the conflicts dividing them about football. It may have done that for only one night, but it was a night not to forget. In those hours of mourning, pro football became a community again. The word has been twisted and misused in American society, but this was an honest-to-God community. These were the faces of pro football speaking from TV studios around the country, to multitudes of football watchers in front of their screens. All were bound in a remembrance of an extraordinary athlete and a good man.

Walter Payton

Communities don't have to last to the end of time. Sometimes they are united for only a few hours or a few days. This one will last in the shared affection of that day.

What was different? Here was a football player whose death could reach a harsh and willful man like Mike Ditka and others like him, and touch them with humility. It could reach stoical and undemonstrative football men like Bud Grant, and touch them with tenderness. It could reach an uncompromising competitor like Mike Singletary, and touch him with peace.

Payton was a marvelous football player, and also a decent human being, though he was also known for his streaks of intramural mischief. He was greeted with such unanimous fondness by his peers that they called him "Sweetness," both during his days on the field and after he retired.

No one who rode with him in a car or was victimized by some of his loony locker-room pranks is going to call Walter Payton a saint. But what his peers saw in him the day of his death, and what they tried to express, came to this: When you looked at Payton as an athlete and as a life, you found about the best this game is going to be. He made other players proud to share the fraternity of pro football with him.

They could see his commitment on every play and in every game and in every side of his life.

On a chilly afternoon in 1975 Walter Payton came to Metropolitan Stadium just north of the farm fields in outer Bloomington. He was a rookie then. The Vikings' defense more or less suffocated everything in sight in those years. It had Alan Page, Jim Marshall, Carl Eller, Jeff Siemon, Wally Hilgenberg, Paul Krause and all their familiar accomplices. The team had squared off against the Pittsburgh Steelers in the Super Bowl the previous winter. Most of the fans had never heard of the Bears' Walter Payton.

Almost from the beginning of that game, Walter tore into and around the Viking heavyweights. He piled up the yards and he had the bratwurst-munching Met Stadium regulars in the full flight of jitters. He brought the Bears to the edge of winning—and then the rookie running back went to the sidelines for practically the whole fourth quarter. Nobody knew why. In those years there were no chic young women patrolling the sidelines with their microphones and their fur scarves and Fifth Avenue coiffeurs, eavesdropping on the coaches. So the press box was defenseless against the aggressive silence of the Bears' bench. The assumption was that Walter had pulled a muscle, something like that. He hadn't. Payton played the game so hard, fought the Viking All Pros with an outpouring of energy so relentless that he knocked himself out of the game hyperventilating. He could barely breathe. It would happen to him often in the next few years. At the time, it scared the Bears as much as it relieved the Vikings.

Maybe big-time sports have now become so powerful and freighted with money that those who look fondly on the game and its personalities should be conditioned to some of its programmed changes and its madcap media sideshows.

Yet it's the game, after all, that holds the public: it's action, colliding personalities, big stakes, recognizable faces, esoteric strategies and rhetoric, and shrewd production. With or without the Cover 2s, shotguns, wildcats or four wideouts, it remains a compelling game played by highly skilled and powerful athletes. On every play we can expect to see something from the chessboard, something from the battlefield, something from the theater and something from the kids' playground. From the playground? Sure. When you're down to the last play, keep lateralling the ball until something happens. It's what everybody did in school.

And today football is prospering as it never has, though we still have some sort of balance between wealth and egos and the team's best interest—not the tidiest basis for harmony—but that is roughly what we have, and it obviously is working.

Newspaper folk my age are expected to look back nostalgically to a time when there was still a place for confidentially in the writer-player-coach relationships. I won't deny it. I liked spending a couple of hours in a honky tonk listening to Ray Charles with a football coach, Norm Van Brocklin, who was eating himself alive because his inferior football team couldn't win more games. You could do that without sacrificing your commitment to professional coverage, which ultimately included a near fist fight (would you believe?) with the same Norm Van Brocklin. I liked the days when a Paul Flatley might come over in the locker room and say, "I got to tell you what happened last night...and you won't print it, will you?" And I'd say, "No, not until you retire or confess." And it was a deal.

I remember Ed Sharockman and Earsell Mackbee trading blows for five minutes in a blood-smeared fistfight in training camp, and leaving it with enough (if grudging) mutual respect that they never exchanged a hard word the rest of their careers. I remember Mel Triplett crying in rage and helplessness because a coach had cursed him racially and he couldn't, in those years, do anything about it. I remember Bill Brown hitting the line at the end zone with such ferocity that he rammed the goal post stanchion in a half dozen games, coming out with concussions and eventually giving the NFL one of several reasons to move the posts back 10 yards to the end line. I remember Rip Hawkins and Fran Tarkenton alternating a round-the-clock vigil at a Bemidji hospital, praying in behalf of the team for Tom Franckhauser, who was almost killed making a tackle in training camp. I remember Fred Zamberletti, the team's trainer for four decades and now a cherished part of its heritage, speeding the unconscious player to the hospital, working the phones to get the best expert advice available, and in the end, saving Tom Franckhauser's life.

Have the game's changes altered the game's appeal? Some have. What matters more is that some values in the game are still strong. You can still see personal integrity and class in the performers along with their skills, strengths and commitment.

Long before he won the Super Bowl, Tony Dungy's Tampa Bay team lost in the last minutes to St. Louis in a playoff game that could have put his team into the championship. It was a television moment I'll never forget. When the game was over, Dungy did not wave to Dick Vermeil, the winning coach, and vanish. Nor did he make the simple, obligatory handshake and walk away, morose and crushed. Rather, he embraced Vermeil in an unmistakably gesture of honest congratulations, talked with him civilly, professionally and personally.

And then he waited until the victorious Rams walked past and congratulated them individually. There was no bathos or contrived chivalry in all of that. It's the kind of person this man is. And of course the entire football world, years later, discovered the human being Tony Dungy is—in victory, in the grief of his son's suicide, and in his depth and public service as well as his success as a coach.

Watching Tony Dungy in defeat that Saturday afternoon, I remembered that he had played and coached in Minnesota, collegiately and professionally. I've known a thousand Minnesota athletes or athletes who played here. I don't know when I've admired one more.

For all of its convulsions and its clashes of money and ego, football is still a game. At times the passion it receives from its fans is comical in its intensity, but there are times when its drama is genuine and moving, and then it is worth the audience it has created.

In the midst of all of the show, it's easy to overlook the humanity in the game, and the remarkable personal character of some of the men who play it. Bud Grant, for one, put huge stock in finding and holding on to players of character. I don't think it was a coincidence that the Vikings of the late 1960s and the 1970s and later were led by players like Alan Page, who became a state Supreme Court judge; Tarkenton, who became a walking conglomerate after football; Jeff Siemon, who became a minister; Fred Cox, who built three chiropractic clinics; Paul Krause, who went into public service; the charismatic Matt Blair; Chuck Foreman who went into business; Jim Lindsey, who became a corporate leader in Arkansas, and Ahmad Rashad, who became a television star. There were more later, of course, but these were people I knew well.

Ahmad was the jewel. His very entrance into the locker room gave it instant vitality and seemed to signal better times ahead for everybody in the place. He was a player of high ability whose personality attracted friendship in every direction. He had an instinct for the camaraderie of the game and a gift for mimicry and storytelling that almost overshadowed his brilliance as a player. I've never met another big-time athlete whose ease of manner and intuitive goodwill so immediately cut across color lines in the locker room, making him equally accessible to black and white, and friend to both.

There was Joe Kapp, the most unlikely of quarterbacks, a gruff ideal of what the game is about. He played with an intermingling of joy and fervor, pugnacity and unsinkable will. Joe was a sourdough of a football player. He trudged where others ran. He bellowed and snorted and laughed in the mud. He had big muscles and scars all over his face from a beer bottle fight in Canada. When he lined up behind center it looked as though the personnel office had made a mistake and picked a bartender to play quarterback.

Even on windless days, his passes fought the air as though dealing with an alien element. They usually lost all semblance of a spiral after ten yards of struggle. But Joe Kapp was one of those studs who never had an identity problem on the field. There was a man named Kapp and there were eleven named the Team, and the eleven were the ones who counted first, last, and forever. He played with a primeval drive, attacking when he ran, flinging jocular insults at the other guy. It was the playground all over again, every play. And because his accomplices included Jim Marshall and Bill Brown and Dale Hackbart, who played the same way, the sourdough quarterback was utterly believable. The team treasured him, droopy passes, homely codes of team play, and all.

Such a player doesn't want to be mobbed by worshiping spectators as he comes off the field, in fact hates it and fights his way through it. The people he wants and needs to share the exhilaration are the ones who share the bruises and exhaustion. There was a hard-to-forget scene in the locker room nearly 40 years ago. Joe Kapp and Carl Eller were advancing toward each other, howling and laughing through volleys of flying adhesive tape after the team had won the National Conference championship. Kapp's face was smeared with mud and Eller's jersey was stained red. They were celebrating each other and the team. The tension was gone, the hill was climbed and this was the release. They were together, winners in a title game. They met in the chaos of half-naked bodies and abandoned helmets. "Joe," the African-American lineman said, hugging the Hispanic-American quarterback, "you're my brother.'

In fact, still is. Whatever comes in the years after, the bond is essentially forever.

Under the money frenzy and show business of today's football, that sense of sacrifice and commitment among players can still be found. And it can be as intense as it was in the earliest years, when they lived out of each other's pockets. The pockets are much deeper today. But for all of the game's visibility and bombast of now, the hunger to share that final yard, for most of the players of today, is as deep as it was then.

Bud Grant is a former head coach of the Minnesota Vikings whose 18 seasons included 11 division titles and four Super Bowl appearances. He was inducted into the National Football League's Hall of Fame in 1994.

Jim Klobuchar is a former columnist with the *Minneapolis Star Tribune* and the author of 23 books. In 2003 he was nominated for a Pulitzer Prize in journalism by the *Christian Science Monitor*.